AGENDA

Retrospectives

AGENDA

CONTENTS

Important news from Administration – Marcus Frederick		6
INTRODUCTION – Patricia McCarthy		7

POEMS

Simon Jenner:	Der'aa Jean Cras Rattigan's Versions	9
Judy Shalan:	A Welsh hillside Dancing the Circle	13
June English:	Pipe Lines	15
Peter Carpenter:	Near Ronda Epithalamion Buddleia	16
Maureen Duffy	Lex Innocentis 697 Tools	19
Christine McNeill:	Spring Wedding dress exhibition	21
Robert Desnos:	The Legacy Translated by **Timothy Adès**	23
Inge Müller:	Ordeal by Fire Translated by **Timothy Adès**	24
Mc. Donald Dixon:	Boarding Trains	25
Roger Elkin:	There's this memory	26

Robert Smith:	At Langemarck	28
Alison Brackenbury:	On guard	29
Leslie Tate:	Lines of Inquiry	30
John Griffin:	Cenotaph	32

ESSAYS

Simon Jenner:	Dreaming Spires – Oxford Poetry in the 1940s	33
Robert Wells:	Bernard Spencer: 'A dramatic situation in some landscape'	43
Andrew McCulloch:	'A State Between': The Poetry of Anne Ridler and E.J. Scovell	55
Peter Dale:	The Renunciation of Poetry: Reflections on Laura Riding's Position	64
William Hayward:	Six poems Introductory note by **Peter Carpenter**	74
Josephine Balmer:	A Genuine Art *The Perfect Order: Selected Poems 1974-2010*, Nasos Vayenas *Selected Poems*, Alejandra Pizarnik, translated by Cecilia Rossi	80

POEMS

Peter Dale:	Labradorescence	84
Robert Wells:	Ionian	85
Robert Hamberger:	Being the Sea	87
Clare Best:	How they are at home How she walks home	88

Matthew Barton:	Fall Snow	90
Jane Lovell:	Snowy Egret	91
Penelope Shuttle:	Single Sleeping-in	93
William Oxley:	Old Gate of Essex	95
Will Stone:	Le Château de Valgenceuse	96
Sue Roe:	Dream of a Dress Radial Space	97
Robin Renwick:	If The Ram	99
John Gladwell:	Measuring Each Angle	101
Mandy Pannett:	Begin with a riddle	102
D.V. Cooke:	The Dance of Death	104

GENERAL ESSAYS

Phil Cohen:	Carrying the Torch? Poetry, Sport and the Cultural Olympiad	106
George Watson:	Commonplaces	119

SIX CHOSEN YOUNG BROADSHEET POETS

William Searle:	The Mute Swan The April Cormorant The Stone Wall	123
Sarah Holland-Batt:	Rosser Park The House on Stilts Poem for my Father at Sanssouci	127

Dom Knox-Crawford:	Dungeness Vileweed Garlic	130
Seán Hewitt:	Speech Therapy From *Presents from Papua* i and ii	133
Ian Harker:	Earthwork Tree Nets	136
Kaddy Benyon:	Palm House Milk Fever Undone	139

ESSAY BY FORMER CHOSEN YOUNG BROADSHEET POET

Zoe Brigley:	Reviewing Neglected Younger Poets Part 1: Mythmakers and Breakers	142

NOTES FOR BROADSHEET POETS

Peter Dale:	The Light is Dark Enough	149

BIOGRAPHIES 155

END PIECE
Bernard Robinson:	I come from ageless mystery	160

Artist on front and back covers:

John Hacker studied Art at Kingston School of Art and later at the Royal College of Art.

He has lectured widely and taught at Epsom College of Art for 21 years, after which he taught at Hornsey College of Art and Kingston College of Art. He also worked for Chicago University on the archaeological drawings of Ramases III in Luxor. He lives in East Sussex where he has his own studio.
www.johnhackerartist.com

Important News from admin@agendapoetry.co.uk

Agenda is to trial a **new via email only submission policy** starting **1st April 2012**. Until further notice where possible, please send each poem in an individual Word document to submissions@agendapoetry.co.uk

There will be a **twelve-week** submission turn around time, during which every effort will be made to reply to your submission. If you have not had a response during this twelve-week period, then we feel it is acceptable and fair to submit your poems elsewhere. Should you already have a snail mail submission with us, please apply this new criteria and submit new work via **email**.

We hope that this trial of accepting submissions **via email only** will save on post and material costs, ease the administration and in turn speed up the process of reply.

Please go to the **submissions page** at www.agendapoetry.co.uk for further details and guidelines.

Agenda will now be sending out regular **free newsletters** via email, which will keep you up to date with the latest news, events, special offers and details of forthcoming *Agenda* Magazines and *Agenda* Editions (separate collections of poetry). It will also provide a link to our new easy **online subscription** facility using **Paypal** at www.agendapoetry.co.uk plus links to other areas of the Agenda website such as the **submissions page** and the new *Agenda* **online bookshop** where back issues of the magazine and *Agenda* Editions can be purchased.

Any queries regarding subscriptions, book orders or any other administra-tive matters should be e-mailed to Marcus Frederick (Fred) at admin@agendapoetry.co.uk

Personal emails for Patricia McCarthy should be sent to editor@agendapoetry.co.uk

Agenda now has its own **Agendapoetry Facebook** page and **Agenda Twitter** account and buttons for these are integrated into the *Agenda* newsletter and website to enable you to follow us. We hope you will add us to your own pages and thereby keep us informed of all your latest news, views and photos. Over the coming months links to other social media sites such as You Tube will give access to film and audio clips of *Agenda* poets reading their work.

We look forward to developing these internet-based facilities that enable us to produce a vibrant website archived by the **Bodleian Library, Oxford**, and as always an internationally acclaimed poetry journal.

Marcus Frederick
Administration Manager

Introduction

Neglect has always been the bane of poets, novelists and artists. Who knows how many poets, particularly women poets who were condemned to silence, to no education, or to hiding behind their men, have been buried in an undeserved oblivion, never even reaching the printed page?
Gerard Manley Hopkins defines the tortured state of neglect in one of his dark sonnets:

...This to hoard unheard,
Heard unheeded, leaves me a lonely began.

In this issue *Agenda,* takes a good look, both retrospective and prospective, at undeservedly neglected poets of the not too distant past and also in the present. The poets focused upon that hail mainly from the 30s, 40s and 50s include Bernard Spencer, Sidney Keyes, Anne Ridler, E.J. Scovell, A.S.J. Tessimond (who is shown to be the young Peter Dale's 'curious gateway to modernism' in his essay in the Notes for Broadsheet Poets), Laura Riding, William Hayward and the Argentinian short-lived poetess, Alejandra Pizarnik. Distinguished critics/essayists have contributed, along with a vibrant mixture of new, established and lesser-known voices. Essays on other neglected poets such as Thomas Blackburn, Anna Wickham, Clere Parsons will appear on Agenda's website www.agendapoetry.co.uk so keep a look out for them.
The first clutch of poems is linked by the theme of war, mostly the Second World War – which ties in with the era of most of the selected neglected poets in the first group of essays.
For those of you especially interested in the poetry of the 30s, *Agenda* brought out a special Auden/MacNeice issue, Lauds, Vol 43, Nos 2-3, some copies of which are still available.
To counterbalance the first half of this issue, the second half concentrates on new young voices from England, Wales, Ireland and the U.S., invoking a future of a singing poetry that will endure despite fads and fashions. To illustrate this, the work of six chosen young poets is highlighted. Also, Zoe Brigley, herself a former young chosen *Agenda* Broadsheet poet and now a highly-regarded established poet with a second collection, *Conquest* (Bloodaxe, 2012), to her name, assesses a host of young Broadsheet poets who have gone on to have collections published. She has divided her survey into three parts and the first part, 'Myth-makers,' is featured here.
The next issue of *Agenda* focuses on more undeservedly neglected Celtic poets, mainly from Ireland and Scotland as well as some surprises. (A

Welsh issue of *Agenda*, 'Carpenters of Song', Vol 44, Nos 2-3, came out in Spring, 2009). This is to be followed by an issue on the theme of 'Exiles' or 'Refugees', linking in with the Cultural Olympiad so articulately and topically discussed here in Phil Cohen's essay, 'Carrying the Torch? Poetry, Sport and the Cultural Olympiad'.

Many thanks to all our contributors, readers, and subscribers. In these hard times, please encourage friends to subscribe to *Agenda* to be uplifted, inspired, intrigued, comforted and challenged. Poetry needs its champions more than ever now, and gives back its own undying support to the human psyche in whatever age or place.

Let us end with Gerard Manley Hopkins again who, in a bleak depression, dubs himself 'Time's eunuch', in contrast to the birds that 'build'. It is to be hoped that those of you who write poetry, as well as the undeservedly neglected poets, never have to bemoan the fact that you do not 'breed one word that wakes'. The 'word that wakes' is a difficult enough aim, yet many such words are to be found in these pages!

Patricia McCarthy

Simon Jenner

Der'aa

And shall I set down this:
that in Der'aa once – it wasn't.
A sweet uncircumcised sturdy man
who I loved whipped me; from
intimate weals I striped blood to Damascus.
Night-chilled, the scars look down.

Not on my bone-pale flesh, but on white
ribbed sands of Arabia was I
the outrager. I was never caught ,
defiled by a Bey. Turks, atrocious
carriers of their competence
never bloodied this blaze of earth like me.

Me, lying of Der'aa, lying straight through
the gritted teeth of the dead.
Weals to the back they'd understand,
my men; wounds to it, never.
Nor loss of face, led by the nose to snatch
a Syria carved by Sykes/Piquot.

I too was a bleached skeleton by the end,
failed gambitting with blood, made –
against the grain of Bedouin goodwill –
whole countries merely red. Death drank
into sand, obeyed me: made my loves
the shat black jets on a camel trail.

We couldn't meet now, he who scourged
my barren ecstasy. I deserved not more
than humiliation from later pliant lads
on the cusp of a yawn with just a skin
of his fathom, who would cherish each
spasm he raised there better than my soul.

It's that mews boy now, or Rev Boanerges
till I'm snow-blind in the sun;
lean forward, into him in his litre flare
as he whips, kisses my face
thrashes hard, who'll pulp me one day,
leave me dead, anointed in his oily wake.

Jean Cras

(1879-1932)

My telescope eye's still good for Cyclops;
the Mediterranean's eye for eye. In this
tenebrous alignment of glass, Polytheme,
your singularity owes nothing to sight.

Your bale look threw pitiless eloquence
back at stars, but burned inward
into eruptions, magmas of who's blind.
How delicate you cusped Galatea.

You'd not wonder how I scored you then:
operatic bass, tenor, soprano cream
in staves lapping as I hove round
my torpedo squadron to her lover.

Odysseus might covet my killer tracks
parallel as bars of treble clefs. French
from the shrieked steel as Boche cruisers burn.
our low boats pounced their roaring blind.

Searchlights splintered; they split in two.
It wasn't them I homed on, my cabin
privy to battle with horns,
low through a tremolo fog of cellos.

I sunk my way to medals, an Admiral's
brass section. I could not pierce to you
your tongue unknowable as Phoenician,
your soft palate rasps in my brass essay.

Solitary, I felt the swivel of your pain
how making a fist of it you snarled
intricate nothings of lovers with bile
a reflux of tenderness swallowed for an age.

They squint me here from Brittany,
the binocular Paris Opera for this hulking hat.
How delicate the matelot transposes howls.
How he stares past you as he launches his eyes.

Rattigan's Versions

This roadkill view of the world –
fresh pressed flesh into the pot
I never count in the adventures
of my stomach. These kitchen sinkers

should try fresh tail gunner. They tried me
but I was long marinated *entre deux guerres*
pickled to my 0.5 Browning versions.
Now these war children evacuees from taste

miss-aim for me. All's blurted,
scatters to anger's great coagulant.
I saw tragedy's perfect arc punch tracer.
In icy trajectories I fell to my own.

Piffle. I saw tragoidia as goat song too:
jetted test pilots out of the dead and back.
I mean laughter, inexorable as plot,
to twist monosyllables with tears.

Devastate with tact. In my world whispers kill.
Not jewelled precision, just craft: a cuff links' flash
at dawn when your young lover deserts you.
Silence haunts hangings more than tenements.

Pauses. Act Two positions. Or the call
to fray your eyebrows before the half.
The flayed look worth three monologues.
That committed position on tears.

Judy Shalan

A Welsh hillside

Forget if you can the suicide bombs and collateral screams,
Ice warnings from television screens.
Remember instead a day in June
When two sides came from a bend in the road
To a hillside in Wales.

East and west gathered there unsure where the day would go.
He guided them through step by step.
And though Chapel himself he found other words.
And when each daughter spoke of love
He helped them along. A nod, and a nod.

Remember how he then went back
To part the curtains again
For a brother needing more words from Islam.
How that single note caught their breath
And they were warmed by the telling.

Dancing the Circle

First one, then another drawn in,
Left over right, right under left
Holding the silhouette round a centred glow.

A step to the left, a step to the right
Forward close forward, sway, sway.
Thalassa pulls, eddies and flows
The Aegean wind calling

To a Celtic memory in the fire
As the warm band binds.
Forward cross side, behind cross side,
There at the start, there at the end
Bending the vine in and out.

Across and across, turn.
To Turkey, Romania, Russia's Steppes
Israel ya habibi Palestine.
Back close forward to the Yemenite
Forward and back again.

They weave along the labyrinth
Swinging arms up and up
Till chiaroscuro's gentle tone
Calls them in for a healing hug
And stop. Still. And turn.

Note:
'ya habibi': darling or friend – Arabic words heard in an Israeli dance.

June English

Pipe Lines

Thirteen Roosevelt Road –
there was something about that house

from the moment you stepped inside,
hungry for the steak pie, baking
in the black-leaded Kitchener; breathed
in lavender polish rising from lino floors,
that, when mingled with Old Holborn puffed
from Dad's pipe, spelt home.

*

Look, that's him, sitting in his velvet armchair
puffing his pipe. He's chanced his usual Saturday
half-crown on the 'donkeys,' a five race accumulator –
and the first three have won. That's me and our Jim,
sitting on the edge of the settee, yelling,

Come on, *Homeward Bound*. Come on ...

eyes glued to the fourteen-inch telly
watching every black and white movement,
screaming our hearts out, yelling He's gonna do
it Dad. Look he's up front –

You've won Dad, You've won,
and him shouting, Four down. One to go –
don't count yer bloody chickens, wait
fer 'em to hatch.

Sixty-five pounds he won.
New shirts and frocks all round –
what a knees-up we had! Sofa and chairs
pushed to the walls, carpet up. Grandad,
strumming his banjo, Mum on the piano.
Awful how it all slides away, dissolves

into Dad's empty pipe, set down
on the hearth of a house
he never saw...

Peter Carpenter

Near Ronda

He came here to breathe –
to live that way must have been
his determination.
Trace a finger through dust
on the marble-topped chest –
from the master bedroom,
crutch-angled, the legs
of two easels, rust-splashed.
Behind stringed piles
of *The Listener*
canvasses face into one
another. A gecko scuttles
across the baked terrace.
Squint into the light
he worked from
a nailed tautness to these
as it took his breath away.
Drawers are wedged
with mauves and lemons,
oxidised solid in their tubes –
a brush you expect to give
flicks against your thumb-nail
brittle as fish-bone.
It used to swim
with the movements
of wind through leaves.

Epithalamion

'Teach me to pray on this side of the frontier, here where the woods are.'
                                                            Thomas Merton

You're both crossing over the border now:
you looked at her, she looked at you – that's how
you arrived here – right time, right place.
Those rings are a charm, like a rose or a cross,
sure as a promise, symbols of grace.

You're both crossing over the border now:
you looked at him, he looked at you – that's how
we all got here – right place, right time.
Those rings are a charm, like a cross or a rose,
like a tune that sticks, a perfect full rhyme.

Like a perfect full rhyme, a tune that sticks,
those rings are a charm, like a rose or a cross,
to bring back a look, a touch, a kiss.

You're both crossing over the border now:
like a perfect full rhyme, a tune that sticks,
that moment of meeting, a touch, a kiss,
sure as a promise, a symbol of grace –
rings on your fingers, right time, right place –
you called us to witness your shared act of faith.

Buddleia

You stuck on in there, just doing that age-old
'Awkward Squad' job, in garage forecourts,
deserted sidings, under scaffolding, in lots
fresh-earthed by economic crisis, padlocked
and guard-dogged. You must be certificated
in security defiance, bowing, wise and pendulous,
only a fraction to the police presence and looters
as London Road goes up in flames, or there in
tourist-trap cobbled dead-end city waterfronts,
you defy scythe and trimmer, survive 'Attacken',
there even after island killings, Scandinavia
to Thurrock, hanging out with die-hards, ragwort,
wild fennel, it's your pollenated mauve snouts
I still pick out, shading to brown, come mid-August.

Maureen Duffy

Lex Innocentis 697

When Adomnan laid down his law, calling together
the princes and the warriors, that the deaths
of civilians, women and children, non-combatants
should be paid for in blood money, wergild
(compensation our half-hearted word) the law
of the innocent in that seventh century we dub
the Dark Ages, he appointed guardians
overseers to make it stick. So when my aunt
my mother's sister was killed by a stray nazi
bomb she'd have had a hide of land, a couple
of goats, her weight in gold, by rights, in those
barbarous times. And the thousands now in our
civilised century brought out from rubbished homes
laid in mute rows like bundles of old carpet
some longer, some childishly small, what should
their price be, beyond the dreams of avarice?
Only these bitter fruit, enough to make a saint weep.

Tools

My uncle Jack of all trades brought back from France
the candlesticks he'd crafted from German shell-
cases that grace my table, and carpentered
from mahogany off-cuts the little box
harbouring my spare fuses, whose lid sockets
perfectly into its brown body. Now I have
his tools: whetstone, box plane, chisel and the pocket
set he carried: bradawl, gimlet, screwdriver
in their leather case stamped, 'Handyman', with
the arms of Scarborough town, picked up
on some seaside holiday. But not
those others: trenching iron, flogging hammer
and the 'pom-pom' that deadened his bloodless fingers
as he punched out the guts of old steam boilers
filling his gas-tattered lungs with soot till
he spat black phlegm into the kitchen sink.

Today seeing the rack of ancient tools
old gardeners sweated over, hand crafted
I can see his hands, pocked with shrapnel stains
yet delicate to pick out a hair fine
herring-bone or finger a blade for sharpness
before he stropped it on the moistened whetstone
darkened wet slate, penknife or spade, honed
to carve or slice London dirt, or weld
at work with soldering iron, spirits of salt
and molten silver, the colour of his hair.

Christine McNeill

Spring

He stands in his Sunday best,
showing off the top hat
decorated with spring flowers,
with ribbons and small fruit
given to those Austrians
about to serve in the First World War.

Beside him his uniformed comrades, proud,
as if carrying all they have lived to an altar;
not knowing that the ripening fields
in another country would be littered
with dead bodies and that soon
they would be among them.

A homing pigeon is caught in the photo.
I see it flying up the hill, alight on a branch,
swoop away in an arc
as if showing him the slow way up
to where it all ends
for the wider view –

blinds drawn on the windows at home.
Walls will record his mother's grief.
And somewhere outdoors in minus two
a robin will summon spring:
untroubled by the dying light, it will fire up its throat:
will only stop when the dark is complete.

Wedding dress exhibition

Midnight-blue velvet
laid out a step above where years before
her husband's coffin stood.

Once a curtain her mother had sewn,
sometimes dropping needle and thread
to rush to safety from an air raid.

People wander past her
to the dress next to hers,
white silk, five years old, a couturier's.

January gale. Her hat had held.
Pictures taken in black and white.

Sunlight lays an unearthly veil on the stone floor,
the crucifix, the altar;
turns silence into blooming spaces.

A photographer trains his lens at those saints
whose colours spill out in rainbow hues,
landing in painterly strokes

on the ancient, the cold. The sun is a living
god she wants to push away,
but it twins her to what it wants to say.

The happy-day smiles not supposed to end.
The long walk back up the aisle.

Robert Desnos

France 1900-45

The Legacy

(1943: posters say Victor Hugo would back the régime)

Hugo! So here's your name on every wall!
Deep in the Pantheon, turn in your grave,
And ask: who's done this? Hitler! Goebbels! They've
Done it, the guttersnipes: Pétain, Laval,

Bonnard, Brinon: accomplished traitors all,
High on the hog. They've done it, and they must
Face retribution, merciless and just;
And there are not that many names at all.

These mindless and uncultured men have made
A smokescreen for their filthy escapade:
'The fellow's dead and gone,' apparently.

The fellow's dead. Yet his bequest is clear:
His legacy is signed and proven here,
Witnessed by France; we call it Liberty.

Translated by **Timothy Adès**

© *Editions Gallimard*

appeared 14 July 1943 in L'Honneur des Poètes
and in Ce Cœur qui Haïssait la Guerre, *1944*

Inge Müller

1925-66

Ordeal by Fire

Fuhrer's order: the German woman does
Not smoke. (DANZIG MENACED BY RUSSIANS.)
Females born '25, the paper says,
Must honour their obligations.

The Propaganda Minister spat
Sixteen lines in praise of The Girls.
In the smoke and flak of Berlin's ack-ack,
In the ordeal by fire, who falls?...

Hanna Preus, 20, soldier's wife.
Four weeks she'd been with her soldier.
She'd sworn to be true to the colours for life,
Wearing field-grey, at the altar.

Elvira, a warden, her surname was Klaus,
Sole child of a coal stockholder.
Seventeen, says the gravestone near their house:
She'd gone and enlisted as older.

Anna Simon, who cried, before she died,
'Who's stitched us up, betrayed us?
I never was one for an ack-ack gun,
Never wanted to join the soldiers.'

Four dead girls, one hadn't a face,
Laid out by the gunnery crew.
One soldier took for a souvenir
A bloodsoaked feminine shoe.

Translated by **Timothy Adès**

Note: Ack-ack: anti-aircraft

Inge Müller, *Wenn Ich Schon Sterben Muss* published by kind permission of
© Aufbau Verlag GmbH & Co. KG, Berlin 1985

Mc. Donald Dixon

Boarding Trains

Beware boarding trains at unmarked stops,
in the middle of nowhere. Headstones
shell-shocked, defy a Mauser's muzzle
poked at your ribs to prod you forward.

An obscure photograph taken on
Agfa film, by an SS officer
inside a ghetto, somewhere in Europe –
no doubt – the year 1944

Scrolled in black and white on faces, old
yet young, registering signs bereft
of living – bereft of joy, except
for a smile, sneering at the tracks…

They ride the cattle trains to Auschwitz,
road signs betray the next stop. The world
did not care then, or now, once quick bucks
can be made, trading propaganda.

Somewhere on a plane to Europe, I met
a woman with a number tattooed
on her arm. She is proof. There was Dachau,
Buchenwald, Belsen and Auschwitz,

Wherever else she and others congregate
against their will; whether in a gulag
or Gitmo, railing at wars that never
end. Like the scars on her body, they thrive

on tattoos, or numbers on headstones
gone faint like my head on a spliff,
the pain of thinking too fast – fodder, or
memory, boarding trains at unmarked stops.

Roger Elkin

There's this memory

of you. Little big-man,
your parting straight as if it's been ruled;
your medallion face, shining. The rest
of you, a compromise. Shirt freed
from collar, cuffs rolled up,
braces sagging, dangling,
your trousers' top-button undone,
and you're sitting, square-set
but comfortable at the scrubbed scullery table
while Gran's out of your way, clattering
at something deep in the kitchen.
In front of you, the chicken frame,
collapsed, empty wreck of itself.
This is Sunday evening, and you've
put away your workday face, have lost
that churchy-important verger look,
and you're you: Granddad. Full-on.
All smiles. Fingers in the chicken frame,
dibbing, licking glistening lips, and sucking.
Lifting gizzard, and mouthing it
as if it were the harmonica you're trying
your best to get a tune from. Enjoying it.
Getting stuck in, down to the bone,
the chicken grease sleeking up your
cheeks, your skin – and, suddenly,
your eyes give signs you're aware
of my staring. *If this were Russia*,
is what they say, but without need
for words. You've come through the vacuities
of trench, the slitherings and founderings
of mates, the thirties and their hunger pangs,
the second war, Belsen and the bomb,
and this is Sunday, after all, in your
after-life. And *Yes*, you say, *Yes*.

That's good. Then pile the chicken bones
to a bonfire pile, and wipe your fingers
on your handkerchief, carefully,
carefully, as if there's still time.

Robert Smith

At Langemarck

Only the round
of the solitary paths

to mark these dead,
the wind anguished, towering
in the trees,

droning the afternoon
across the plain of Flanders,
its bent hectares;

the divisions
allocated here, called in
from a honed salient,

their names,
inscribed, the dates
under a tainted sky

blackening over time;
the language borne on sufferance,
a rebuked silence –

Note:

German war dead (1914-18) buried in the Ypres salient were later exhumed by order of the Belgian government and reburied in mass graves in a single cemetery.

Alison Brackenbury

On guard

My father, aged nineteen, tramps Dusseldorf,
no tourist, guards the military HQ,
brown curls crammed in his cap, gun scoured, in view
as the top brass roars into Dusseldorf,
raw shrapnel in his neck, false teeth on gums,
from forests where the wild boar fled from guns.

At night the staff cars sweep from Dusseldorf.
Past the stone houses, down the cobbled street
the Sergeant Major limps on stockinged feet,
'Don't shoot, you bloody fool!' as Dusseldorf
freezes, my father's rifle trains his head,
his rations heap a hungry Fräulein's bed.

What, in the icy dawn of Dusseldorf,
shoots a sharp rustle from the broken hedge?
The sentry, bruised, sprawls in the gutter's edge.

A German Shepherd, Nazi Dusseldorf's,
breathes over him. Instructed once to trip,
now starving, she remembered her old trick,

awaits his orders. Whistled, in hills' white space
through frost, low sun, his father's sheepdogs race,
quick Choc, soft Toots. She licks his frozen face.

Leslie Tate

Lines of Inquiry

Granny Piano with Grandpa Tenor and seaside choir
rehearsed it in the living room with a candle.

Barefaced with a pipe, his father's father,
winking in the mirror, cheated playing cards.

Dared by a sixpence the little boy ran
to await the all clear
when his grandmother banged murder
on the locked pantry door.

She forgave him in her heart
when, blinking back tears, he used the wind as alibi.

All afternoon the head down fathers
defended the front room
testing their LPs and homemade equipment,
holed up in passion with the Berlin Philharmonic.

Then eyes down, a tempo, paced out the beach
to the Ninth, the Unfinished, Ein Deutsches Requiem.

Great aunts and uncles were studied for resemblances
caught unawares as they peered from albums
of suited page boys, nurse cadets,
and riders in uniform kneeling with a grin.

Now sheeted into hush
the boy's undercover pretending not to hear
with torchlight trained on *Boy's Own* adventures
to put aside wishes hidden in his bed.

Behind him now the all-eyes show
when, standing tall, he sang sweet Jesus,
old beyond his years, appealing for their love.

Then deep and dreamless and washed to a sweat
as he shivered to Our Father, remembering the pain
crying in the chair while feeling for his parents
when, chewing on delight, his loose tooth hurt.

To give all for his mother, gazing into dark
as they walk in step to the memorial gardens
where silence hymns the dead
with blackout, fidgets and two-minute warnings
to remember who they were
– while downstairs, alone, playing for time
his father's smoking
following the wood grain in the tall-backed chair
to retrace victory on a map.

John Griffin

Cenotaph

A shell sounds and sea bones tremble. There are deeps
within the deep where even the waters are drowned,
swallowed up by the heft of their own interminable dark.

You may think a rhythm can dredge sense from absence
or salvage water from water, or you may think the dregs
of memory can restore what's lost from what is thought.

Here's the sand where the blood of hope seeped away
and there the tides tolled their bells of foam into waves
that broke along the years and then sank back to silence.

Simon Jenner

Dreaming Spires – Oxford Poetry in the 1940s

On or about November 2nd 1941, British poetry changed. An overkill, a publicity stunt even. But literary history can be altered by literary accidents – and personalities. *Eight Oxford Poets,* edited by Sidney Keyes, went to press without Philip Larkin. It began a feud with the mostly posthumous Keyes lasting forty years and fissuring the perception of a whole poetic decade. Keyes's neo-romantic stance fuelled his antipathy to the then Audenesque Larkin. It also made him highly influential, so particularly reviled by Larkin. Writing to Robert Conquest on the latter's prospective inauguration of *New Lines* and Movement. Larkin was fuelled mostly by – as late as 1955 – a desire to revenge himself on 'our Sidney', (to Norman Iles). Larkin's animosity against Keyes enshrined the Forties for him. It fuelled Larkin's bid at recognition in another decade, that might underwrite his existence. Without him the Movement might appear what for many it has always seemed: a journalist-manufactured and limiting prescription, a kind of literary Beveridge Report. The Forties neo-romantic myth was summarised in Thomas. Yet when the Thomas-admiring Larkin wrote to Conquest, the poet scapegoated for Forties 'excess' was unequivocally, always, Keyes.

The trouble with the Forties is that it ended in 1945. Cauterising the decade's poetry into its first five years was understandable for obvious reasons. But the traumas and dramas have receded; the writing remains. Opening the buff envelope at both ends – the Thirties as well as the late Forties and Fifties – points to a very different achievement: one of continuity and more than foreshadowing. The finest new poets of the 1940s emerge as not really Forties poets at all.

Keith Douglas, Sidney Keyes, Drummond Allison... Larkin, who like Allison would live in Belfast, writes in a similarly Audenesque manner, to 1943. It astonishingly prophesied his later maturity with just such a feeling for deracination, and in the same imagery he would later reinform it with. The Forties clearly formed him as a writer, and his mature poetry in one sense offers an oblique elegy for those permanently deracinated by psychological upheaval or simply death. Larkin, seeking Yeatsian closures not gleaned from Auden, ironically absorbed the same influence as Keyes, with similarly mixed results. It is an accident of literary history that Larkin's Yeatsian period, and not his on the whole finer Audenesque one, was available to readers for more than twenty years longer.

Larkin aside, straddling both periods, the best poetry of the Forties does seem now more forward-looking, and incisive than much Movement poetry. It vitally transmitted to later poets like Geoffrey Hill the poetic intelligence, contemporaneity, verbal excitement, metric virtuosity so dominant in the 1930s. This places Larkin in such an exciting context.

Universities offer a deferred oblivion to precocious talents spurred by their imminent death. In fact Oxford saw (or spawned) much of the most enduring poetry of the war period, including that of Douglas, Allison, Keyes and the early Larkin, and stands in an altogether more ambiguous relation to the poetry of the 1930s. And it is significant – though hardly surprising, this being Oxford – that Auden's influence is detectable in all, modified (not muffled) by war's charged circumstances. Wartime presaged more than apocalpyse or last-ditch romanticism. Its deadpan dislocations fulfilled several 1930s prophesies in verse. These, and the techniques they accessed, struck many of the most intelligent and incisive of the later poets, as fit models for a provisional island.

This Oxford group included writers as diverse as Heath-Stubbs, David Wright, Michael Meyer, Amis, Alan Ross, and Geoffrey Matthews, as well as the four above-mentioned poets. During and after the war this remarkable succession continued with Elizabeth Jennings (the presiding genius), Christopher Middleton, Al Alvarez, John Longrigg, Martin Seymour-Smith, William Bell and Geoffrey Hill. Some indication of their own strong group identity should be made, not least because several were very sympathetic to the older poets. Hill for instance was influenced by Keyes and championed Douglas.

Allison, Douglas, Keyes and the early Larkin were the most important members of this loosely-associated earlier group. Postponement, deferral, deracination, anxiety at looming annihilation: these themes and motifs mark them all. Much of their poetry – particularly Allison's – transmitted an elegiac continuation of Thirties modernist procedures, modified by the fact of war and political betrayal. Of the four, only Larkin survived. This fact tends to obscure the links between his early verse and that of his Oxford contemporaries. The point is that Larkin himself did his best to suppress it in one of the most strangely influential spats of literary pique in 20th century literature.

*

For this distortion it is necessary to pass over the supremacy of Douglas and Allison to consider the effect of another poet, in many ways their equal, for long thought their superior. Keyes was aptly named for his extraneous importance as a war poet whose best work – 'Poem from the North' recalled his friend Allison's and Auden's rather than some of his more neo-romantic gestures. Keyes was by contrast to Douglas even better known in Oxford poetry circles, which crystallised in his anthology *Eight Oxford Poets*.[1] Taken on by Routledge, this allowed Keyes access to literary fortune. The anthology set out to proclaim an end to the Audenian school. In its muddled attempts to prove and promote a new Oxonian Romanticism already emergent elsewhere,[2] it embittered some at Oxford, and permanently distorted the poetic reality. And establishing Keyes's romantic persona and influence, did him posthumous harm.

Keyes was lucky with his publisher, Routledge for 46 years, and now Carcanet.[3] Two Routledge volumes fulfilled a public need for romantic gesture, sweeping rhetorical gifts, and a resonant certainty saturated in a vague, florid symbolism; real mythopæic address grounding in striking closures.

An awareness of Continental models was Modernist enough; but in the 1940s, particular poets – the later Eliot, Rilke, Yeats, early Romantics like Hölderlin, offered a war-distracting wholeness, variously deploying symbolism. It's redolent in the Eliot of the *Four Quartets*, in extreme forms with the Apocalyptic movement,[4] and even implicitly in for instance the critical work of Louis MacNeice on W.B. Yeats,[5] as Heath-Stubbs for one registered.

Keyes's precocity, fluency, mastery of the striking phrase, his romantic affiliations, made him ideal iconic material. He was what was needed, and his reputation has suffered for it. But Keyes's attitude to romanticism did shift from his own pronouncements. This might not be helped by Meyer's assertion in his stimulating memoirs *Not Prince Hamlet* (1988) that Keyes will be seen as ultimately a 'bigger poet' than Larkin. The context illuminates official literary history. Meyer grumbles that Larkin only accorded Keyes

---

[1] *Eight Oxford Poets,* ed. Sidney Keyes and Michael Meyer, London, Routledge, 1941. (Publication date 2 November – see Meyer, *Not Prince Hamlet,* p. 44, below).

[2] For instance, in the work of Thomas, Barker, Gascoyne and others. The later 1930s had seen the rise of such groups as the Apocalyptics, led by Henry Treece, and J. F. Hendry. Much of this can be seen as a reaction to the omnipotence of Macspaunday. More specifically, since many of these poets sympathised with the socialist credos of the earlier group, it recorded political disenchantment. They, too, remembered Spain.

[3] I refer here to the 1962 reprint, and 1988/2002 revised *Collected Poems*, still edited by Michael Meyer.

[4] Although Henry Treece is synonymous with the Apocalyptic school, it was J. F. Hendry who in fact wrote most of its polemics. A.T. Tolley discusses this in *The Poetry of the Forties,* Ch. 7 'Apocalypse and After', especially pp. 109-110.

[5] Louis MacNeice, *W.B. Yeats,* London, Faber 1941.

'a single page of Keyes's poems in his *Oxford Book of Twentieth-Century English Verse.*' It was perhaps bigger of Larkin to include a page of Keyes at the time he did, for as Meyer elsewhere recalls, Keyes excluded Larkin from his own anthology *Eight Oxford Poets*, which included work by Keyes himself, Meyer, Heath-Stubbs, Allison, Keith Douglas, Gordon Swaine, Roy Porter and J. A. Shaw. Those omitted included Larkin, John Mortimer and Francis King.

It is piquant too that Keyes's personal liking for Allison led to the latter's very Audenesque poetry being included, whilst Larkin's was not. And it was impossible to exclude the very un-romantic Douglas, almost *hors concours* for any Oxford anthology then. His work too kins far more with Larkin and Allison than Keyes and Heath-Stubbs. Despite apologias by Heath-Stubbs, the possibility of personal dislike, or more of poetics, remains. Larkin would weigh as one more Audenesque poet in an anthology designed to prove an opposite neo-romanticism. *Eight Oxford Poets* was altogether a mixed metaphor of a selection, and its results have been out of all proportion to its importance, even given the talents of those involved.

*

Keyes in his Foreword proclaimed: 'We have, on the whole, little sympathy with the Audenian school of poets,[6] Keyes, as a TLS reviewer pointed out, was writing against the evidence. Keyes's Foreword is disingenuous, including such 'Audenians' as Shaw, Allison, and Douglas. Meyer's poetry too, was still 'under the spell of Auden.'[7] Their Audenesque poetry compromised it already, as quotations from reviews above show.[8] 'Our Sidney' Keyes might well have approved of Larkin's Yeatsian *The North Ship*, had he lived to read it. But the pre-1943 Larkin in his poems identified with Keyes's 'Audenian school'.[9] He defended the use of 'good' Auden against the 'bad' of *Another Time* – already distinguishing between the 'English' and later Auden. This would have placed him with Douglas and Allison, whom he liked personally.

Had Larkin been included in Keyes's *Eight Oxford Poets*, the latter's neo-romantic Foreword would have collapsed. Larkin was where Keyes drew his winter line. It became the fracture whereby Larkin, embittered and of his own

---

[6] Meyer, *Not Prince Hamlet,* quote from Foreword to *Eight Oxford Poets,* p. 44.
[7] Meyer, *John Heath-Stubbs in the Forties,* pp. 179 - 87.
[8] Meyer, *Not Prince Hamlet,* p. 44.
[9] *Eight Oxford Poets,* ed. Keyes and Meyer, Foreword. Quoted by Meyer, *Not Prince Hamlet,* p. 44

volition, seemed forever part of a later poetic period.

Heath-Stubbs recalls: 'Larkin never forgave Sidney for this omission, and in later years spared no opportunity of attacking his memory.'[10] Anthony Thwaite, the editor of Larkin's letters, stated that Larkin 'always maintained that Keyes had excluded him from the book.'[11] Amis concurs. 'Philip was not represented; it appears since that Keyes, who might have known that Philip considered him a third-rate personage, left him out with some deliberation.'[12] Larkin's biographer, Andrew Motion, suggests:

> He continued to grumble about Keyes... The only memory of meeting him that he chose to preserve was one in which Keyes 'was wearing a bloody silly fur hat and had smelly breath.'[13]

Perhaps in selecting two of Keyes's poems in 1972, Larkin was burying his own hatchet in his own infinitely more prestigious anthology, possibly with a vicarious pleasure in doing better by Keyes than the latter had by him. Perhaps there was some operative guilt, as Edna Longley has suggested. The manufactured fault-line between Forties and Fifties poetry runs across the antagonism between these two poets.

It was Keyes's ideological stance that fuelled his antipathy to the then Audenesque Larkin. It also made him temporarily highly influential, so particularly reviled by Larkin, as for instance when writing to Robert Conquest on the latter's prospective inauguration of *New Lines* and the Movement. Larkin was fuelled not so much by a new polemics in poetry, but – as late as 1955 – a desire to revenge himself on 'our Sidney', as he once referred to him.[14] Certainly Larkin had no antipathy to, for instance Dylan Thomas, whom, as his *Selected Letters* makes clear, he always admired, as much as did his 'Movement' friend John Wain.[15] His long friendship too with another neo-romantic, Vernon Watkins, is well known. Ironically, Keyes would have preferred the Yeatsian Larkin of 1943-44, an extraordinary (if temporary) fulfilment of Keyes's more romantic programme.

---

[10] Heath-Stubbs, Hindsights, Ch. 5, p. 84.

[11] Philip Larkin, *Selected Letters of Philip Larkin,* edited by Anthony Thwaite, London, Faber, 1992, p. 26 n.

[12] Kingsley Amis, *Memoirs*, London: Hutchinson, 1991. 'Philip Larkin', p. 55

[13] Andrew Motion, *Philip Larkin: A Writer's Life,* London, Faber, 1993. Six. p. 45.

[14] ibid. To Norman Iles, 7 April 1942, p. 34.

[15] ibid. pp. 28, 46, 55, 79, 133, 218n, 260, 264, 292, 303, 342, 345, 373, 378, 447, 660, 662, 754, 758. Admiration ranged from the adulatory to the occasionally critical. A note of asperity is only introduced when writing of Thomas to the more disapproving Amis. e.g. To Kingsley Amis, 11 January 1947, p. 133.

Keyes's Forties was specifically what Larkin wanted to repudiate in the mid-Fifties. In Larkin's *Selected Letters,* this, to Amis and Conquest over at least forty years, emerges clearly:

> What does annoy me is reading shit by Sidney Keyes wherever I turn... You pick up any two bob pocket magazine... & you'll find bullshitty poems or tossy 'Short Stories' all by our Sidney. I wouldn't mind if the man were any good but in my eyes at least he's absolutely crap all use & I am gnawed by pangs of jealousy. 'Sidney Keyes is already outstanding' says Stephen Spender in the Year's Poetry in Horizon... He can make four thousand a year & edit his own paper but he'll still be a sodding bad poet. (To Norman Iles, 7 April 1942)

> Yesterday I saw a book with 'The Complete Poems of Sidney Keyes...' printed on the outside. They want fifteen shillings for it and they can go on wanting as far as I am concerned. (To Kingsley Amis, 9 August 1945)

> I think you are quite right in stressing the poor quality of poetry during the war – a period which can laud the poetry of Keyes is no period for me... (To Robert Conquest, 28 May 1955)

> And of course death is the great irresponsibility (sIdNeY kEyEs Is DaFt). (To Robert Conquest, 26 April 1956)

> I'm glad he {Clive James} has no time for Keyes or Roethke, both entire phonies in my view... (To Anthony Thwaite, 21 May 1974)

> I reckon Heaney and Co. are like where we came in – Keyes, Heath-Stubbs, Allison, Porter, Meyer. Boring too-clever stuff, litty and 'historical.' (To Kingsley Amis, 21 November 1982)

That he should rate the twenty year old Keyes as 'phoney' as late as 1974, is remarkable. Significantly, the only time he softened towards Keyes was in 1944 – with the latter recently dead. Larkin reluctantly, admits:

> I *still* don't like him. He has been getting smashing reviews, comparing him to Keats... But I do admire the way it's a long time before you notice he doesn't rhyme hardly at all. That is an admirable feature, & an accomplishment I envy... (To Norman Iles, 16 April 1944).

Larkin owns to being 'gnawed by pangs of jealousy'. This directly fed his encouragement of Conquest's ambitions. Larkin's admiration for Thomas and Watkins was balanced by a dislike of Keyes, but also by a disavowal of Conquest's promotion of future 'Movement' poets. Notwithstanding his caveats on Conquest's equally 'literary' 'Movement' Larkin applauded the opportunity to repudiate the Forties. If it could praise Keyes then 'it is no period for me.'

More to the point, it had not praised Larkin. Such rancour has point; *Eight Oxford Poets* served several contributors well.[16] Keyes and Heath-Stubbs went to Routledge; Allison, posthumously, only to the Fortune Press (in 1944), as did Larkin.

*

Larkin's part in reshaping the received notions of Forties poetry, was proportionate to his increasing influence as the most highly-regarded post-war poet.

As Meyer suggested,[17] and as Larkin's own letters prove,[18] Larkin never forgave Keyes for this. In 1955 he demonstrated how acute his and Conquest's sense of periodising were, stating emphatically: 'A period which can laud the poetry of Keyes is no period for me.'[19] This is ironic: the decade had seen a greater creativity, and even publication, than he was ever to achieve again. In his introduction to *Jill,* Larkin admits that possibly Bruce Montgomery was the stimulus: 'for the next three years we were in fairly constant contact, and I wrote continuously as never before or since.'[20] His two superb novels *Jill* and *A Girl in Winter* display a greater maturity in prose than *The North Ship* does in poetry. Despite this, Larkin subsequently distanced himself from the Oxford Forties as decisively as he could. This occluded Larkin's Forties origins as an Audenesque poet amongst others like him – Allison, Douglas, and Ross. And, because the Forties meant 'Keyes' to Larkin, he was keen to promote the antipathetic myth of Keyes's version of a neo-

---

[16] Meyer, *Not Prince Hamlet,* pp. 55-6. Keyes, in a letter to Meyer of 26 March 1943, from Algiers (en route to the Tunisian campaign) comments gleefully: 'I consider myself 8 Oxford Poets' front line!' This is very possibly a pun on his now overseas status. He had been 8 Oxford Poets' front line poetically and politically, well before that, and knew it.

[17] Meyer, *Not Prince Hamlet,* p. 44.

[18] Larkin, *Selected Letters,* e. g. To Robert Conquest 28 May 1955, and 28 April 1956, pp. 241/260. Previously discussed in chapter on Keyes.

[19] ibid. p. 241.

[20] Larkin, *Jill,* Introduction, p. 19.

romantic Oxford when corresponding with Robert Conquest. The effect of this perceived fracture, which Larkin himself did much to promote, cannot be overemphasised.

*

> In 1946 or so I went and stayed with him... My chief memory is reading a .. typescript, book of his early, unpublished poems. . . {These} evoked Auden, though not at all directly... *The North Ship*.. left {me} rather cold.. it was these poems that he had never published that told me how good he was and would be.[21] Kingsley Amis, *Memoirs*

Only in 1988, with the publication of his *Collected Poems*, did the Larkin of official literary history begin to acquire a sepia period tint of his own. The Amis of 'Letter to Elisabeth' and 'Belgian Winter' was being unduly modest about his own achievements to 1946 – but was right about the quality of these early poems, over those of *The North Ship*.

Larkin had not simply polemicised a particular early version of himself: he had suppressed his very interesting, precocious Audenesque poetry, dating from when he described reading Auden's Airman as 'like being allowed a half-hour telephone conversation with God.'[22] Even when it was published, not even Hamilton[23] really drew the connection between Larkin and his contemporaries, any more than anyone had really dared do with the 1946 Yeatsian collection *The North Ship*, republished in 1966.

That collection might with a terrible irony have placed him with Keyes. Larkin's preface, however, claimed a famous solitary discovery (and thieving) of a Yeats volume.[24] This occurred in the girl's school he was librarian to in 1943 after Oxford. It fits the myth of a schism between his early and mature styles. It also shrouds a still earlier style that when juxtaposed with his Yeatsian period, illuminates his poetic maturity. His anxious appending to the collection of the 1946 poem 'Waiting for Breakfast' did little to dispel this, itself still Yeatsian.

Thus far literary history records Larkin's disjunction from the poetry of Oxford contemporaries, courtesy of Keyes and Larkin himself. More than

---

[21] Amis, *Memoirs*, 'Philip Larkin', p. 56
[22] Larkin, Auden, The Orators: 'The Airman', quoted by Ian Sampsom, Radio 3, April 2nd, 1999.
[23] Ian Hamilton, 'Phil the Lark', *Times Literary Supplement*, 18th December, 1988
[24] Philip Larkin, *The North Ship*, Preface, p. vii London, Faber, 1966

this dissociation from his past, is Larkin's apparently unique deracination in Belfast into a lone individualist, emerging into the dim meritocracy of the Fifties. He's himself transformed into a British poetic metaphor for isolationism; an icon of the Movement.

From 1966 to 1988, an eccentric but unexpectedly important sliver of Larkin's poetic development – *The North Ship* – only seemed to prove Larkin's sudden poetic maturing in Belfast, around 1950. Perhaps republication of the two novels might have signalled a far keener critical intelligence than this volume displayed: they seemed so creatively at odds with it. The mature Larkin can now be seen to have drawn the two earlier selves together: Audenesque particularity (adjectival phrases, for instance), tone, verse forms, conversation pieces; and Yeatsian grandiloquence in his closures.

This Audenesque had emerged gradually; very early work – such as 'There is no language of destruction,' yield a purer Auden fingerprinting, with the startlingly dissonant adjective, as in: 'Silence the only/ Path for those hysterical and lonely.' "The Schoolmaster" 'prepared for the long years to come/ That he saw, stretching like aisles of stone/ Before him.'[25] Suitably modulated, this language was the Larkin of, for instance, 'Coming'[26] with the thrush's 'fresh-peeled voice/ Astonishing the brickwork.' It also employs the Skeltonesque short lines that Graves and Auden so championed and used to such effect.

The general virtuosity of metre, rhyme, and syntax bespeak a thorough grounding in the Thirties revival of these. The Auden of 'As I Walked Out One Evening' with crowds like 'fields of harvest wheat' shelves into 'postal districts packed like squares of wheat.' The last simile is one of several in 'The Whitsun Weddings' that re-enact the observer's mobility in some of Auden's pre-war work. By 1957-58, the time of writing 'The Whitsun Weddings', it was fully assimilated. 'Mr Bleaney', apart from producing Audenesque echoes in 'incomplete unrest', also learns from Auden in its complex syntactical handling of adverbial phrases.

The later influence of Hardy (according to Larkin, from around 1946)[27] was a patina. It steadied the despair, but Hardy could not have encouraged the ringing Yeatsian closures ('Nothing, and is nowhere, and is endless'), the vivid Audenesque particularity ('postal districts packed like squares of wheat'), or knowingness ('a *Which*-fed argument').[28] Larkin's tone lacks

---

[25] Larkin, *Collected Poems*, p. 248
[26] ibid. p. 33
[27] Larkin, *The North Ship*, p. vii
[28] Respectively, 'High Windows', 'The Whitsun Weddings', and 'The Dance'.

Hardy's humility, though not generosity – allowing a certain narrowing of this. Poems of tenderness towards women are perhaps the most infused with this spirit. These would include 'Love Songs in Age', 'Talking in Bed' and perhaps most movingly, 'Dublinesque'. Larkin's melancholy found an apt corollary in Hardy's. But his mature voice has much in common with Auden's, and in drawing broad-canvassed conclusions, Yeats too. The material to thus assess the poetry was unavailable till 1988.

*

Inheriting Auden's earlier manner, and perhaps even more temperamentally in need of a textual closure, Larkin apprenticed himself to a master of such rhetoric with a greater cunning than Auden, with his spun-out cultural and personal gestures. Thus Larkin's texts resolve themselves (partly with earlier selves) with a greater if incomplete satisfaction. The price was a certain narrowing of tone, outlook, and willingness to take risks that so distinguishes (say) Douglas's poetry. It might too throw some light on Larkin's inability to write novels after the 1940s. Social upheavals and confrontations are enshrined both in his two novels and the period generally. They contained elements the mature Larkin might well have found disturbing in his increasing conservatism, being in themselves more difficult to avoid in prose than poetry.

Larkin's alien sense of provisionality that emerges so early and often in these poems sought a kind of grounding in rhetorical clinches. This sense would enlarge from chilled bedsits to a particularised elsewhere lent by Auden and underlined through Yeats, to a more fulfilled tone. This has previously seemed one that was finally liberated by Hardy. Yet that tone had been previously packed into the Audenesque metaphor.

The choice of naming one's personal tradition sets up a discourse – in this case a public and influential one. Larkin named his false start with Yeats so suddenly and simplistically replaced by Hardy. In 1978 he faintly rocked that 1966 version of his earlier development. Publishing 'Femmes Damnées' was a wry admission of one slipped persona briefly flashing another, pretending ignorance of *doceur* or *bêtises*. A bit Stratford atte Balls. The polemic grimace of the 1950s was decisively dropped with the publication of the *Collected Poems* in 1988. This – instead of the promised variorum – was redacted into a shrunken head, a canonic *Collected*. Larkin's whole output has been waiting for a decent period since.

Robert Wells

Bernard Spencer: 'A dramatic situation in some landscape'

The most immediately attractive quality of Bernard Spencer's poetry is its openness to the world, to the look and sound and feel of things. Its guiding principle is, in his phrase, 'respect for the Object'. Its subject-matter he defined as 'a dramatic situation in some landscape', adding 'I need to get the background and, so to speak, the furniture in, even some small details.' (There is a likeness and a debt, here, to Thomas Hardy.) Inclusive as he is, Spencer selects and constructs like a draftsman, so that though he sometimes dwells on scenes of clutter – the untidy deck of a cargo boat, the loaded merchandise on the back of a donkey – the writing remains spare. The cargo boat displays in its 'swerving planks' 'the sea-shape simple and true like a vase'; the ankles of the donkey under its pyramidal load 'are tiny like children's wrists.' The poems have a strong paraphraseable prose content, yet we soon become aware of a hidden pull beneath the clear surface (in Lawrence Durrell's phrase, 'a weird specific gravity'). For Spencer a poem arises when he detects 'the twist in the plotting'. The twists are many, but the pattern of the drama is unchanging. Typically the vividly rendered moment leads back to some earlier, much less clearly apprehended scene, and then to a barrier. The poems approach the barrier with mixed feelings of longing and fear. And it turns out that the present scene, though it has – as it must – its own reality, is a substitute or cipher for something unrecapturable, the physical experience of some lost place and life which lies 'ages back in the hardly waking mind'.

'Yachts on the Nile', from which this line is taken, is one of the poems in which the pattern reveals itself most directly. Here is the full stanza:

> Terrible their perfection: and theirs I saw
> like clouds covering the Solent
> when I was a boy: and all those sails that dip
> ages back in the hardly waking mind;
> white visitors of islands,
> runners on the turf of rivers.

The present moment, as the yachts are observed entering a race, leads back to a childhood memory which is more indefinite ('like clouds') and then to remoter recollections which a full stop and the close of the stanza cut short. Fear ('Terrible their perfection') is in tension with longing, implied in the opening of the previous stanza ('Lovely will be their hesitant leaving of/ the shore for the full stream') which mimics the movement of the poet's meditation, as, following the yachts, it too moves out from the shore to 'the full stream.' The scene described is at once immediate and remote. The race holds the yachts 'like a legend'; the Nile is a by-word for antiquity. Other poems which clearly show the passage from precise present to impalpable past and to a blankness, beyond which something forgotten but still powerful lies unreachably concealed, are: 'In Athens' ('there is given/neither name nor time, except it was long ago:/the scene, half-caught, then blurred'), 'By a Breakwater' ('a sometimes blurred, other times emerging query,//Almost recognition') and 'The Empire Clock'. Elsewhere the pattern appears more obliquely and incompletely in the situation and imagery of the poem. But it remains a constant.

Behind the alert clarity of response which distinguishes Spencer's poetry and gives it its enduring freshness, there is, we may infer, a story or 'dramatic situation' of his own for which the situations represented serve as analogies, and which will help to account for a body of work at once so unencumbered by egotism and so personal. Spencer's poems of travel are never merely unattached impressions. He comes upon his subjects by chance (the luck, in one of its guises, invoked in the title of the second of Spencer's two books of poems, *With Luck Lasting*), but he chooses them, or rather, they choose him, for a reason. What, then, determines the choice? Spencer was a child of Empire. 'For me,' he declared, 'poetry begins very much at home, wherever home may be'.[1] But where was home? Born in 1909 in Madras, Spencer was separated from his parents and sent back to England shortly before his second birthday. Kipling, in his autobiographical story 'Baa Baa, Black Sheep', describes what it might mean to be thrust into this category of 'strangers' children', who 'through no fault of their own had lost all their world.' For Kipling's protagonist, the boy Punch, the loss occurs at the age of five. Spencer's poetry contains no mention of India (apart from a passing reference to 'an Indian goddess' in an uncollected undergraduate poem). Yet the loss for him at the earlier age was the more irremediable because it lay beyond memory. Life for him had to begin over again, marked by a consciousness that he came from elsewhere, that a long voyage separated him from the place to which he once belonged[2]. This is the burden of the lines which close 'Yachts on the Nile':

and it may be, too, we are born with some nostalgia
to make the migration of sails
and wings a crying matter.

The beauty of these lines lies partly in the ambiguity of their syntax. If we imagine a stop after 'sails', where the line break makes a pause, the sense is that we have an innate need to migrate, returning – the yachts are 'like birds' – to the place from which we come. Reading on, we discover that 'make' is not used absolutely but has a predicate, and that the journey has to do with grief and poetry. 'A crying matter' means not only a cause for weeping but a subject-matter which cries out for expression. Kipling in his story links Punch's loss with a precocious compensatory passion for language. Spencer remarks on a similar precocity in himself: 'I used to pray that I should be a traveller abroad when I grew up, just as I used to pray that I should be a poet.' For him the two wishes are inseparable, committing him to a quest for a reality to replace the one taken from him. 'The poet's immoderate, promiscuous love'('Acre') has its origin in an immense deprivation.

It happens that two of Spencer's principal champions, Lawrence Durrell and Alan Ross, the editor and publisher of the first *Collected Poems*, were themselves born in India and sent back to England. Ross records the event (he was seven at the time) and his intense grief in his memoir *Blindfold Games*, where he also cites Kipling's story, lighting on the phrase 'strangers' children'. 'The childhood' he writes 'is real though scarcely remembered, as if memory itself was blindfolded' (p.19). In fact, as his memoir indicates, Ross recalls quite a lot – like Kipling he returned to India later, and he made it the subject for many poems. But for Spencer the blindfold is of a kind that can never be taken off. In a poetry where the visual sense predominates, he makes many references to blindness. In 'Egyptian Delta' 'the powerful ox' (it is harnessed to a water wheel) 'with dancer's step goes round,/and his lifted eyes bound.' In 'In the Beginning', his only poem about a non-contemporary historical event, Spencer writes of the castle which, once built, brought about the fall of Constantinople to the Turks, and so 'changed maps, slew thousands, put out like an eye/world-renowned mural work of crowns and thrones and wings.' In both poems blindness is associated with some more general effacement; in the first, positively (because deprivation accepted, not repined at, opens the way from an inner poverty to a surrounding plenty), with 'an excellence of losing track,/of being no longer a person or sad'; in the second, disastrously, with the loss to the Greek world, cherished by Spencer, of its capital, and with the destruction of a civilization.

Spencer is drawn to archaeological digs and classical sites as scenes of vanished empire, an unknowable past; as evidence, too, of the kind for which he is always looking in both present and past, of 'the permanence of the basic things of a life' ('Greek Excavations'). In a sketch of landscape, 'Near Aranjuez', he notices 'a crumbling tower' and comments 'there was once/ something forgotten now to love, to guard.' An instance of effacement from more recent history is treated in 'An Empire Clock'. Other poems in which Spencer returns to the theme are 'Delos' ('the boulevards of these dead'), and 'Delicate Grasses'. In the second of these, longing and fear are matched as they were in 'Yachts on the Nile', but more explicitly. The 'strong liberation' promised by the once-thronged, now-deserted scenes evoked in the poem gives way to the chill of 'one thought further still,' and to the apprehension of a trap. Spencer was puzzled by his poem, and tells an anecdote about it: 'What is the trap? What was I afraid of? Later, at his request, I read the poem out to a fellow-poet, John Betjeman, and he cried out "Oh! Eternity!"'. 'That', Spencer comments, 'is as good an answer as any.' To go 'one thought further' may be to enter the effacement and be caught there, not to be able to get back. The barrier which lay for Spencer at the start of life, dividing him from his infancy, re-forms itself ahead of him, becomes the death which the future, for all its promise, somewhere contains.

There is a varying tension between the experience of loss that constantly returns upon Spencer, threatening to undo him, and the resolution to make good the loss.[3] The recovered reality is a simulacrum of the reality lost, but at moments the fit appears perfect, and it is the sufficiency of what has been found which prevails. The title[4] of Spencer's first book, *Aegean Islands*, emblematizes the irreducible nature of such moments and of the happiness – brief and intermittent as it is – which they bring with them:

> The dark bread
> The island wine and the sweet dishes;
> All these were elements in a happiness
> More distant now than any date like '40,
> A.D. or B.C., ever can express.

More often, though, Spencer feels himself condemned to observe as a foreigner. The more lifelike the substitute, the more by paradox he is reminded that it is not the original. He confronts the paradox in 'Notes by a Foreigner', where, after some exact vignettes of a city, he speaks of his 'wish to build them all/into one vision,' and discovers the wish to be 'illusion'. Addressing himself, he concludes that 'There is just/a sense in which your town never/was true,' and then homes in on his intimation of the truth that is missing:[5]

> The echo-light no town
> (of this at least you are sure) can parallel;
> when things mean more yet fade, like places
> you half remember, a now-not-beating bell.

Things begin to 'mean more' and the ciphers to reveal themselves just at the moment that they become inapprehensible. 'Delos' concludes (with reference to an oracle), 'And it was here by the breakers/That strangers asked for the truth.' Spencer travels in the knowledge that the closest he can come to the truth he is after is to identify those places where the truth can be asked for, where it means something to put the question. Spencer greatly admired the Metaphysical poets, George Herbert being his favourite among them;[6] and (though there is no religious attachment in Spencer beyond residual loyalty[7] to a Christianity inseparable from European culture) his own sense of the visible world as furnishing a set of hieroglyphs by which a hidden world might be intuited is akin to theirs.

This polarity in Spencer's poetry – a tension between all that makes for being and all that makes for non-being – declares itself in other related ways. There is a horror of cold winds and freezing weather which runs from 'A Cold Night' ('Thick wool is muslin tonight, and the wire/wind scorches stone-cold colder'), through 'Base Town' ('The wind savaging from the stony valleys' – the winter of the poem matched to the debasement of war which is glanced at in the punning title) and 'The Lottery Sellers' ('a wind savage out of Tartar places'), to the bitter Viennese winter of 'The Empire Clock' and 'Properties of Snow'. Alongside this, an antidote, there is a counter-imagery of Mediterranean heat and colour – 'violence of sun and its worship,' 'the peacock sea,' 'dazing lion-light,' 'gold-of-wine of morning,' summer 'bolt-shot with perfume, leaf and juice,' the donkey who 'belongs under a blow-torch sky.' In another contrast revealing Spenser's hunger sensually and verbally to lay hold of things, situations are often represented in terms of poverty and wealth. This preoccupation reaches from the early 'Allotments: April' ('real poverty/The sour doorways of the poor') to the last poem Spencer wrote, 'To Piers Spencer, five months old'. Here, addressing his infant son, he notes the boy's first attempts to mouth words, associating this with the impulse to poetry – and so with the literal poverty which is the poet's usual lot, as well as with the metaphorical wealth which the poet's mumbling 'mimic speech' promises. The poem, which has a valedictory tenderness of tone, is itself a gift to his son, a kind of covert bequest from the poet 'short of pence', exemplifying the wealth he does possess. It is the only poem of Spencer's to carry a dedication. Spencer's concern with the 'behaviour of money' receives its most direct expression in the poem of that title. It shows itself too in his fascination with the transactions of trade, as in 'Delos', the island which served as a marketplace ('Floors where the Greek sea-captains piled up money'), 'Sarcophagi' ('twenty-six bargain-makers of Phoenicia'), 'Boat Poem' ('great booming barrels of wine from the mainland/ endearing trade,' and 'On a Carved Axle-Piece from a Sicilian Cart' ('long muscat grapes/or tangerines for the market in the town'). Since trade consists in the supplying of a lack, in substituting a commodity in which you are poor for another in which you are rich, it serves, on the reading here proposed, as a metaphor for Spencer's deepest concerns. His opposites mix and meet and turn into each other. The city, for all its routine solidity, is a place of 'frequent phantoms.' Olive trees contain both 'the cold thing' and 'the warm thing.' The Aegean island rich in 'elements of a happiness' is a barren outcrop. The street-seller of lottery tickets, who 'hugs a rag suit to his chest/on a cold hell's corner,' personifies the wealth he promises. Spencer's poetry keeps track of the instability, catching it accurately in its many forms.

'The twist in the plotting' also turns on the relation between what is accidental and what is determined, between the random detail and the ominous sign. *With Luck Lasting*, not quite the hopeful title it seems, though the hope (and gratitude) are there, conceals a conditional clause and begs the question of the nature of the luck. Numbers are often mentioned, 'a street number to find,' the registration code of a boat (a line added to 'Boat Poem' between magazine and book publication), a sheaf of lottery tickets 'with their potent numbers,' the 'cries of "Two" or "Six"' of bowls-players. In this respect the most uncanny of the poems is 'A Number', an anecdote about a set of coincidences attached to the number fifty-three, which is haunted (or is it?) by an absent final line. Spencer died in an accident at the age of fifty-three. That is what the poem appears, with hindsight, to lead up to, and cannot say. It actually ends with a separated line added by Spencer after the birth of his son, and obliquely referring to it ('When she visited a clinic, later, her room was Fifty Three'). Spencer's wife Anne is shown knitting as the poem opens, and the inference may be that she is preparing garments for the baby soon to arrive. But the poem also refers to 'the Fates at their woolly occupations' and to 'the scaffold in the French Revolution.' Here, as very mutedly in the poem to his infant son, it seems that a birth entails a death. Spencer is at last standing behind the barrier which has divided him from his own lost infancy, as a cycle approaches completion. This is to spell out what exists in the poems as the merest suggestion, unarticulated, perhaps hardly thought. Yet it is striking that in a much earlier poem, 'My Sister', a death, that of Spencer's father, is associated with pregnancy and birth ('My sister great with child, and the old man dying upstairs').The accident in which Spencer died was unforeseeable, but in the later poems there are many such presentiments that a denouement was near. Spencer vanished one evening from the clinic in Vienna, to which, in a state of delirium, he had been admitted after the sudden worsening of an unidentified illness. The next morning he was found dead beside a suburban railway track, having apparently been struck by a train. His shoes were worn out, and he must have walked some distance. In his delirium he had been possessed by the conviction that he needed to return to India. It is hard to resist the conclusion that this is what he was attempting to do, and that, with the constraint of reason lifted away, the 'bare bones of motive' ('Night-time: Starting to Write') which underlie his work are revealed.[8] The circumstances of his death suggest that behind an appearance of waywardness he was a driven, even a fated man. The detached tone of the poetry only lightly covers the intentness of preoccupation which unites it. For Spencer, the advent of a poem was the visitation of an 'Unknown, Demon, what you will.'[9] If the interpretation of his poetry as the attempted making good of an original loss has validity, then the Demon driving him becomes identifiable as his effaced past, rising up against him and demanding realization.

Spencer's nostalgia is also an expectation: what lies inaccessibly behind him perhaps also lies ahead, in some reconfigured form, on 'the road of foreboding and of dreadful hope.' In his search for a world in some way continuous with the one he has lost (it is here that his poetry chiefly touches us, since the deprivation which the circumstances of his childhood made peculiarly his is an acute form of a general condition) he is drawn to 'the different life/that is always the same,' as he describes it in 'The Boats' – a primary life of the senses governed by unchanging human needs. This life he discovers in the local 'vernacular' peasant cultures of the Mediterranean which are celebrated in such poems as 'Aegean Islands 1940-41', 'On a Carved Axle-Piece from a Sicilian Cart' and 'Peasant Festival'. It is the more eagerly reached for because it is under imminent threat. It is 'The life the generals and the bankers cheat' ('Greek Excavations'), or again, where 'being is dirtied by a banker's thumb' ('Cairo Restaurant'). It is the life undermined, as he writes in the poem on the Sicilian cart, by

those metaphysical gaps and fears
which drain the blood of the age or drive it mad;
the 'why are we guilty?' and the 'who must punish?'

These questions lead, for Spencer, into his version of Matthew Arnold's 'strange disease of modern life,' in the poems 'Train to Work' and 'Fluted Armour' (with the echo in its last line of the last line of Seferis's 'The King of Asine'). It was in stepping beyond these anxieties as they dominated the England of the Nineteen-Thirties, and departing for Greece, that Spencer came into his own as a poet.[10] His poems of the Thirties are, taken together, a disappointingly meagre and unrealized group (the chief exception is 'Part of Plenty' – here Spencer has a positive to set against the negative, and this releases him.) In *Aegean Islands* as originally printed they were consigned to a section at the end of the book. First came the poems of Spencer's sudden maturity, written in Greece and Egypt. The book opens with éclat, an effect lost in the three editions of the collected poems, which reverse the order and restore the chronology.

Spencer's celebration carries conviction because his nostalgia has nothing facile about it. By virtue of their nostalgia his poems are true to their historical moment, and lead us towards it even as they would lead us away. They could not have been written at any other time. Both sections of *Aegean Islands* are emphatically dated, and so too (pointing to invasion and displacement) is the title poem 'Aegean Islands 1940-41'. In Spencer's poetry we watch by glimpses an old Europe, under stress of war and of the changes which follow, in the process of giving way to a new. Here are the villages of peasants and fishermen. But here too is the life restlessly housed in the suburbs of expanding cities – the 'blocks without hope going up' of Nineteen-Fifties Madrid ('Notes by a Foreigner'). Spencer considers this city life in two other Madrid poems, 'From my Window' and 'Mediterranean Suburbs'. Despite great differences of temperament and technique, these poems are not unreminiscent of Pasolini's Roman poems of the same period, as they address the question of what future is taking shape and how 'the wish of the many, their abused trust' ('Greek Excavations') will be met in the new dispensation, riven by social division and unacknowledged trauma. Here is the last stanza of 'From my Window':

> Alone on a building site a watchdog stalks by the fire,
> wooed and repulsed by the jump-away flames, or raises its head
> at a barking that chips a hole in distance.

The watchdog is a projection of the poet himself, watching at his window, intent on what is there and listening for what is to come. 'Mediterranean Suburbs' presents the same, or a similar, scene. There is a building site, there is an unfinished block 'waiting for its history', there are approaching sounds:

> Reject of neighbouring streets, then questioning ours,
> the sad and stammering music of a pipe;
> and now its tall and scarecrow player turns
> the corner like the grotesque of some need
> we had forgotten that we were starving from,
> or promise we have broken. Empty houses,
> houses for next year, evening, restless houses.
> Dressed in a city's shabbiness he walks
> under the wild guess of that new-starred sky.

Who is this rejected figure, so at odds with 'the solid' in 'their heavy homes' of the immediately preceding lines? He walks out of the past ('some need/ we had forgotten'). He has to do with the future ('the wild guess of that new-starred sky'). With his 'sad and stammering music' – a contrast to the expansive singing of 'Peasant Festival', a diminished version of the same song – he too is a projection of the poet, of the poet's deprivation, of the need out of which the poem is made. The 'stammering' brings his music close to speech and reminds us of the mumbling 'mimic speech' of the poet in 'To Piers Spencer'. And as there, as also in 'The Lottery Sellers', the poverty holds out a promise of wealth. The 'stammering music,' like the 'mimic speech,' is something that we find ourselves straining to hear.

The openness to the world of Spencer's poetry is seconded by its formal variety and inventiveness. Spencer believed (it was an idea he took from his friend Seferis) that poems are found – 'are waiting around to be written, perhaps in certain parts of town,' For him this meant finding not only the subject matter of a poem but making some equivalent discovery, small but definite, about the shape of its language, some turn of technique so that the poem should not be quite like any other. Without such a turn – a formal counterpart of 'the twist in the plotting' – there was for Spencer no poem. His poems are never lengths cut from the same cloth. 'In each new poem' he says 'I try to set myself a new technical problem… I have written very little in the same form from one poem to another.'

This search for new possibilities (which allies his work with that of the continental modernists whom he read and on occasion translated) is a tall order, and is one of the reasons why he wrote relatively little. Some of Spencer's poems, including some of the finest, 'Delicate Grasses', 'At Courmayeur', 'At "The Angler"', are in regular stanzas, but he tended to prefer the unstable equilibrium of irregular forms, with an intermittent use of rhyme, or a stringently shapely free verse. There is an unobtrusive wit in the matching of form to subject. In 'By a Breakwater' the pairs of long lines bracketing a short line suggest in their effect on the movement of the poem the groynes running down into the sea and providing a minimum of shelter. Then these lines are broken up, as if by the rough weather of the day, by a disturbed meditation on the scene described. 'Mediterranean Suburbs', with its unfinished buildings, itself has a certain unfinished air about it. 'Letter Home' and 'Written on a Cigarette Packet' are shapely conceits modelled upon casual jottings. 'Lop-sided' displays the 'disproportions accumulating' of the gathering storm which it evokes. In 'Sud-Express', one of Spencer's most striking formal inventions, a train journey, its violent speed, its snatched sights and half-apprehended sounds, is rendered in stanzas of increasing length, juxtaposed with elliptically gnomic single lines, also of increasing length, representing the thoughts and feelings of a departing lover. But to draw attention to these effects is to exaggerate them. The equivalents which Spencer devises are neither superficial nor showy. They come from within the language, and reveal it in some fresh aspect.

Spencer makes skilful use of repetition, a poem suddenly returning on itself, as when, in 'Clemente', he writes of a dead waiter, held in affection for the strength of the drinks he had served, that 'he must have been very much mourned...by many who could never properly have known him,' and then pulls himself up with the question 'What does it mean, to be "known"?' – the suggestion being that however ignorant of each other we may be, we should know enough, as Clemente did, to know that strong drink may be in order. The final line, the waiter's remembered vaunting of himself as 'Clemente who wangles you the cruel drinks,' nicely conveys with its subdued wordplay on the name the paradox of being cruel to be kind. In a poetry as quiet in tone as Spencer's, such touches in details of finish, at one as they are with the construction of the poem, have great effect. Another instance is provided by 'On the Road', of which Spencer wrote: 'the theme is the possibility of entirely perfect and happy episodes in life, although the title implies that they do not usually last very long.' The poem, which was published in the year of the death of Spencer's first wife, Nora, recalls in its first stanza a scene in which 'we two drank in the vine-chinky shade/of harvest France.' The second stanza opens with a repetition, 'We two. And nothing in the whole world was lacking./It is later one realizes...' A tiny, almost unnoticeable shock is registered as the 'two' who share the drink and the life together become, over a line break, the 'one' who afterwards recalls the moment of happiness and realizes his loss. 'Realizes', too, has a double sense. The poem closes with another repetition, as Spencer shows himself trying to repossess the lost reality in the one way he can, by composing the poem:

> It is a lot to say, nothing was lacking;
> river, sun and leaves, and I am making
> words to say 'grapes' and 'her skin'.

The loss of his wife brings back over Spencer the desolation of an original loss. It was indeed a lot for him to say that 'nothing was lacking'.

Acknowledgement:
This piece, with additions, changes and cuts, is based on my review (*The Times Literary Supplement* July 1 2011) of Spencer's *Complete Poetry, Translations & Selected Prose*, edited by Peter Robinson.

Notes:

[1] Spencer's phrasing here is coincidentally very near to that of Elizabeth Bishop in the closing lines of her poem 'Questions of Travel': 'Should we have stayed at home,/wherever home may be?' This points to a resemblance between the two poets. Both are preoccupied with 'questions of travel'. Both write a poetry of description where the sharp specificity of detail remains uncompromised by the strong emblematic or symbolic connotations which are also there. In Bishop, as in Spencer, the eagerness with which the world is reached for arises from deprivation. Like Spencer Bishop was brought up away from home and parents after an early separation.

[2] Boats are the subject of four of Spencer's poems. Somewhere behind these poems is a reminiscence of Flecker's 'The Old Ships', Masefield's 'Cargoes' and perhaps Bridges's 'A Passer-By', all well-known anthology pieces of Spencer's youth. The two boats at the close of Matthew Arnold's 'The Scholar Gipsy', the 'Grecian coaster' and that of the 'Tyrian trader', are also perhaps recalled.

[3] Spencer seems to take a certain guilt upon himself for the loss, his poems being a way of making up for the damage done. What moves him about the Phoenician merchants of 'Sarcophagi' is a bargain kept. 'Everything was paid', he says of them. In 'Sud-Express' it is the breaking of a contract which distresses him: 'Going is a kind of treachery: I own it'. In 'At "The Angler"' he similarly refers to 'our crime of parting'. And in 'Mediterranean Suburbs' the 'need/we had forgotten that we were starving from' is associated with a 'promise we have broken'.

[4] In Spencer's title there may be an echo of the penultimate stanza of 'The Scholar Gipsy': 'The fringes of a southward-facing brow/Among the Aegean isles'. Spencer includes Arnold in a list of the poets he read as a boy, and 'The Scholar Gipsy' may perhaps be overheard elsewhere in his poems. The lines from 'On a Carved Axle-Piece from a Sicilian Cart', quoted above, about 'metaphysical gaps and fears' are reminiscent of Arnold's evocation of 'modern life', and the opposition in Arnold's poem between 'modern life' and the life lived by the Scholar Gipsy has its counterpart in Spencer's poems. A further echo in 'On a Carved Axle-Piece' may be Spencer's 'Palermo towers' for Arnold's 'Oxford towers', and the rhyming there of 'towers' and 'flowers'. Arnold's 'some grave Tyrian trader' may have his equivalent in Spencer's 'some tanned peasant'. Spencer grew up in the country around Oxford and would have been familiar with the landscape of Arnold's poem. When Spencer refers to 'my grassy home' and 'any home river/Or the grass of graves there' we may remember the 'tall grasses' over the Scholar Gipsy's grave and the many mentions of grass elsewhere in Arnold's poem. The movement of the poem, at its close, from England to the Mediterranean would surely have been attractive to Spencer, as -- given his preoccupation with trade -- would have been the figure of the Tyrian trader. None of this is decisive, yet it may be suspected that 'The Scholar Gipsy' was a point of reference for Spencer.

[5] The 'echo-light' has its counterpart, perhaps, in the 'snow-crater light' of 'Full Moon'.

[6] The influence of Herbert, like that of Hardy, is well assimilated in Spencer's work, though it can be intangibly felt. Peter Robinson remarks on Spencer's use of the word 'twist'. The word recurs in four of Herbert's poems, including two of the best known, 'Affliction (I)' and 'The Pearl'. There is a note on Herbert's use of the word in C.A. Patrides, *The English Poems of George Herbert*, p.23. Herbert's 'Love', a poem about lack and the making good of lack, can also perhaps be heard in the words 'so love made it seem...' in 'At "The Angler"'.

[7] But it is striking how Spencer will notice a shrine to the Virgin ('The Café with the Blue Shrine', 'At Courmayeur', 'Peasant Festival'). The Virgin is there by implication in 'Cairo Restaurant', and there are a couple of references in Spencer's scattered prose. There is also the allegorical figure of 'mother-Peace' in 'How Must we Live', a neglected but beautiful early

poem. These references reach back to a childhood deprived of maternal affection.

[8] This phrase recalls 'the early bones' beneath the pyramid in 'Donkey' and the 'comfortless X-ray bones' of 'Blue Arm', as well as the 'anatomy dissected' of 'The Building of the House'.

[9] Like the above, from 'Night-time: Starting to Write'. The phrase 'what you will' suggests a glance at *Twelfth Night*, which the poem's use of the word 'bewitched' tends to confirm (Maria says of Malvolio 'Pray God he be not bewitched'). Spencer perhaps feels a certain embarrassment at being possessed by so stagey a Demon, as if he were a gulled Malvolio aiming too high. Certainly his sense of the actual is matched by a sense of the ghostly. There appears to be a reminiscence of *Hamlet*, the opening scene where the Ghost first appears, in 'Notes by a Foreigner': 'the bell then beating' ('a now-not-beating bell'), 'Stay, illusion' ('illusion, your old failure'), and 'The cock that is the trumpet to the morn'/'It faded on the crowing of the cock' ('as though mad cocks had given the dawn a call...when things mean more yet fade').

[10] We may perhaps infer that the poetic alliance between Spencer and Keith Douglas (Durrell speaks of their making 'common cause' in Cairo) had something to do with the need they shared to leave England and its prevailing poetic climate behind them. Spencer speaks in an interview of a determination to 'cut the cackle', while Douglas writes in a letter of the 'immense bullshitting' of which poetry needed to rid itself.

Andrew McCulloch

'A State Between':
The Poetry of Anne Ridler and E.J. Scovell

The poetry of Anne Ridler (1912-2001), like that of her friend E.J. Scovell (1907-1999), first began to appear during the Second World War: Ridler's *Poems* was published in 1939 while Scovell's debut collection *Shadows of Chrysanthemums* appeared in 1944. Both are essentially sacramental poets and it is not hard to see why, under the pressure of wartime conditions, their verse, often strongly reminiscent of seventeenth century devotional poets such as Traherne and Herbert as well as later religious poets like Manley Hopkins, Charles Williams and T.S. Eliot (for whom Ridler worked as an editor and reader from 1935-40), was so popular. A review of Ridler's collection *The Nine Bright Shiners* in 1944 commended the fact that 'even when her theme is in a sense private and domestic...she brings to it...a sense, immediate and penetrating, of the glory of being,' a sense that 'our footsteps echo in another world.'[1] Equally unsurprising, perhaps, is the fact that once such mortal dangers were over the appetite for religiously-minded poetry began to fade. Certainly after Eliot's death in 1965, her poetry fell from favour – although she continued to work successfully as a librettist and translator of Monteverdi and Mozart operas until well into the 1980s – so that a reviewer could complain of her 1972 collection *Some Time After* about the 'notably unproductive genre in which she continues to work... a post-Eliotic, rhetorical, moralizing and metaphysical vein,'[2] a list of adjectives that neatly captures the widening gap between Ridler's strengths and the poetical alignments of the period. It was not until the publication of her *Collected Poems* by Carcanet in 1994 that it became possible to look afresh at the work of this complex, witty, moving poet, 'as profoundly religious a person as I have ever met,' as Ronald Gordon said in his obituary in *The Independent*,[3] vividly and genuinely aware – like her beloved Traherne – of 'Eternity in all appearances/The holiness of everything that is.' Although Ridler agreed with Kathleen Raine that poets should think of themselves as invisible, both her admirers and those new to her work will be delighted by Carcanet's decision to make the *Collected Poems* – out of print for a number of years – available again as a print-on-demand title.[4]

'In Cornwall' is a fine example of the kind of dynamic equilibrium Ridler characteristically achieves between the revealed universe and an unrevealed God. Language shuttles between this world and another in this effortlessly visionary poem lit by a dazzling luminescence only just beyond the intensity of the everyday. The sea 'seems the bright and easy floor of heaven':

There saints like ships can navigate, and fair
The crops of golden plants like sparkles shine.
And O that we were there.
('In Cornwall')

It is as if – to misquote Pierre Reverdy – 'there is no such thing as God' in Ridler's poetry, 'only proofs of God.'

The sea serves Ridler well. In 'Kirkwall 1942', the first of a series of poems dedicated to a husband away on active service, it becomes an image of separation – an image, that is, in the sense that any part of natural reality loved by the poet is coloured by her fundamentally Christian outlook. The same is true of her debt to other poets: if there is a nod to Donne in the idea that although loneliness makes islands of us love connects us to the human continent, it is not a mere literary borrowing but part of a personal theology that finds sacramental expression in a symbolic grammar that shares the same deep structures as her seventeenth century predecessors but is merely differently construed. The sea is, as it were, the ground of many of Ridler's most productive metaphors, recalling evolutionary and Biblical accounts of the origins of life and coloured by both Classical and Romantic myth and periods spent living on its margins. In 'Views of the North Coast', for example, the centuries of attrition and deposition that account for patterns of human settlement dissolve into the darkness on the face of the waters – part primeval, part Biblical – that frequently lies just beneath her treatment of it. In a characteristically subtle elision, geography slides into theology as 'the unseen monstrous waters pour/In centuries against the crumbling shore.' In 'Romney Marsh' life's 'strange beginnings' are not only suggested by land 'our fathers stole' from the sea but also survive as a race memory in the collective consciousness.

It is not only the sea that summons the epiphanic moment. In 'A Mile From Eden', strong directional winter sunlight turns a snowy wood into a visionary landscape where the poet and her husband walk 'tipsy with too much light.' But again, Ridler ensures that the radiance comes from without – 'On snow even the shadows are white' – before she sees it reflected 'in his eyes/Eyes of the humble hoping for heaven.' It is walking 'in a waste of snows' that reveals 'that power before our eyes':

Which if we learn its usage can
Break up the amber, reverse the sun,
The bird's eye glory to full sight
Bring, and outcasts into delight.
('A Mile From Eden')

The unforced drifting of immanent meaning to the surface of Ridler's poetry is nowhere more apparent or more touching than in 'For a Child Expected' and 'For a Christening' in which the poet's child becomes not so much a metaphor as a sacrament expressing at a secular level the mystery of God's incarnation in Christ. The success of 'For a Child Expected' resides largely in the fact that the natural imagery for which Ridler reaches has a Biblical rightness about it perfectly in keeping with the tone of hushed reverence in which, naturally, she contemplates the miracle of birth so that 'Lovers whose lifted hands are candles in winter/Whose gentle ways like streams in the easy summer/Lying together/For secret setting of a child.../...do better than they know.' A similar combination of self-involvement and self-removal ensures the success of 'For a Christening' which also presents the agency of human love as a conduit for the spread of the Holy Spirit. Having invoked as many blessings as she can on her child, Ridler asks 'may we learn to leave you alone,' a touching recognition of every individual's divine selfhood and one that fills out the Jacobean cadences of the closing couplet with real emotional conviction:

> Life is your lot: you live in God's hand
> In His terrible mercy, world without end.
> ('For a Christening')

Ridler was a lifelong member of the Oxford Bach Choir, an interest that sits well both with her work as a librettist and her abiding fascination with the overlap between art and the divine, what the eye sees and the mind discerns. The epigraph to 'Bach's B Minor Mass', for example, taken from Austin Farrer's 'The Glass of Vision', identifies the difference between seeing with and through the eye: 'Faith discerns not the images but what the images signify: and yet we cannot discern it except *through* the images. We cannot by-pass the images to seize an imageless truth.' Here, it is music that gestures towards the ineffable as it cries 'to the unattainable height/Only through the lung's pressure and the bow's bite.' Elsewhere, the truth is even more 'imageless'. In 'Backgrounds to Italian Paintings: Fifteenth Century' Ridler considers a landscape that seems to be haunted by figures painted out of it, so that:

> The wonder awaits you, cornerwise, but never
> Full in the face; only the background promises
> Seen through the purple cones at the edge of the eye
> And never to be understood
> ('Backgrounds to Italian Paintings: Fifteenth Century')

These absent figures, however, come to stand more tellingly for the presence of the divine than what she calls, in 'Deus Absconditus', 'the junk and treasure of an ancient creed' that we persist in carrying 'To a love who keeps his faith by seeming mute/And deaf, and dead indeed.'

Some of Ridler's most successful poems are those where, indeed, 'wonder awaits you, cornerwise.' In 'Picking Pears' the delicate autumnal vignette is compelling enough on its own terms to hold at bay gathering hints of another kind of fall:

> Nor heaven, nor earth, a state between,
>   Whose walls of leaves
> Weave in a chequer of dark and bright
> The falling sky; whose roofs of green
> Are held by ropes and chains and beams of light
>   ('Picking Pears')

The last line puts Vaughan's theology of blinding light to practical descriptive use so that when, at the end of the poem, the pears are harvested and 'summer's nimbus shrivels on the rind.' It is an aureole of natural light, not a halo, that we imagine around the fruit and with which the poem can continue to glow if we choose to let it.

Ridler is acutely aware, nevertheless, that the balance between the visible world and the divinity with which it appears to bristle can only be achieved by the shaping power of art which consequently, when it fails, threatens the ability to perceive God in Nature. Matters are further complicated by the fact that it was the desire for knowledge that led to the exile from nature it is part of the function of poetry to redress. 'The Images That Hurt' presents the poet as Adam, urged towards an understanding that brings only pain:

> Far too much joy for comfort:
> The images hurt because they won't connect.
> No poem, no possession, therefore pain
>   ('The Images That Hurt')

What lie scattered about in the poet's garden are 'all the materials of a poem' but unless or until she can connect them all they do is reproach her both with her failure and with her inability to live simply amongst them. And when poetry fails so, too, does the struggle to imagine the divine that it attempts to articulate: 'As those who gaze from the cliff at the depth of the sea/And know they cannot possess it, being of the shore.'

Most of the time, of course, not only do the images connect, they do so with an almost Metaphysical combination of delicate feeling and robust dialectic.

'Nothing is Lost', for example, uses 'proofs' from heredity, memory, even cellular regeneration to suggest the immortality of the soul, the final verse moving easily from the opening quasi-empirical 'thus' to a teeming sea of souls on which we float and which will not let us drown:

> Thus what we see, or know,
> Is only a tiny portion, at the best,
> Of the life in which we share; an iceberg's crest
>   Our sunlit present, our partial sense,
>   With deep supporting multitudes below
>   ('Nothing is Lost')

The sense of being 'sustained by powers not my own' becomes a physical feeling in 'Bathing Off Roseland' where the sea, 'a firmament that curves below,' is a reflected heaven on whose floor the poet feels 'lulled and directionless' like a bird – Ridler resists saying 'angel' – 'with all four wings outspread.' Although she drifts on a 'tide of prayer', however, the closing image reminds us that the other-worldly can only be comprehended through this one:

> Another's love can sway me toward
> Some good that of myself I would not:
>   Powerful, hidden to me,
>   As the purpose which drives these great ships forward
>   Parting the sea
>   ('Bathing Off Roseland')

But belief is most convincing where it struggles most honestly with doubt – as Ridler said 'you've got to face the fact of death, that it is an ending; one hopes that it is also a beginning, but you mustn't cheat yourself by believing too easily in that'[5] – and a late poem, 'Free Fall', dramatises this struggle through a description, finely balanced 'between dismay and laughter', of a French tailor who, in 1900, was filmed attempting to fly from the top of the Eiffel Tower in a bat-winged costume he had made himself. 'The wings will surely beat/And bear me up,' he thinks, and yet is understandably reluctant to jump. When he does, 'the lens below/Can barely follow the plummeting shape/So quick his fall.' A 'ridiculous death' perhaps and yet the absurdity of expecting a miracle goes to the heart of all belief which, in the end, requires of 'each in that crowd, and you, reader, and I' a last, lonely leap of faith.

E.J. Scovell was born in the same year as W.H. Auden and Louis MacNeice although her first collection was not published until 1944 when, as she once said modestly, the war had created 'a need, or a liking, for poetry of all kinds.'[6] Not explicitly religious, her poetry nevertheless trembles with gentle affirmations, finding 'depth or luminousness or what seems a kind of intensity of existence...in the object.'[7] She would not describe her outlook as religious, she said, unless 'religious experience and aesthetic experience were the same thing'[8] which in her view was not the case. 'The nearest I get to religious belief,' she added, 'is that I can't imagine anything existing without being in someone's consciousness...without being apprehended.'[9] This central concern of her work is well caught in 'Agnostic' in which she speaks of her relationship, as strong as the one between believers and their God, with 'This life and world apart from me.../In whose silence most I see/A calling soul, calling my scrutiny.' The world's 'silence' makes the bond with the poet 'strong and deep and torturing and fond' and also, paradoxically, guarantees her spiritual honesty. As she said, 'if I did believe anything definite I would *ipso facto* disbelieve it. I would think "we can't know."'[10]

This attention to the way 'the mild surface scene hums with its deep' ('Fragility of Happiness') is particularly evident in the gently meditative 'The Evening Garden', the first of Scovell's poems to come to the attention of John Mole who, with fellow poet Peter Scupham, published a pamphlet of her work, *Listening to Collared Doves*, in 1986.[11] The gentle interplay of opposites in the opening verse, and the rocking, lullaby rhythms, create a dreamy, liminal world in which, when they come, the thresholds of curtains and window pane are dissolved 'in this/one hour when all is seeming':

> Not dark nor light but clear,
> But lucid with no source of light,
> But breathing with no flow of air
> The garden journeys into night
>   ('The Evening Garden')

The garden may, at this hour, be losing its war with the 'shadowy lights in the glass' – which are themselves looking both in and out – but it has 'behind it all the universe' in a moment that recalls the balance achieved by Coleridge in 'Kubla Khan' between the unassailable fecundity of nature and the fashioning powers of art – explicitly, perhaps, in the 'girdling wall' around this 'salient into wild creation.' In 'Bright Margins', thresholds do not so much dissolve as disappear altogether as manuscript and floral margin fuse into a single meaning:

> I thought of decoration such as once was done
> To frame a manuscript – how the finished work is one,
> Cornflowers and gold are one with the marmoreal
> Script...
> ('Bright Margins')

This idea swells, in the second verse, into a similar coalescence of the natural world and the language in which poetry attempts to capture it, as real flowers seem 'the silk of thread/Not woven in the cloth, embroideries, not the words/Nor the meaning of the words; and still the work is one.' This sense of meandering inclusiveness is helped by the fact that a single sentence threads its way through the poem's twelve lines: even the stanza break is a line early (after line five) leaving the second verse to begin with a trailing tendril of sub-clause, an echo, perhaps, of those cursive patterns where 'firm and sounding Latin words' tail off into fantastic calligraphic invention.

A different kind of bright margin is the subject of 'The Stream Bank' where 'all strands that reach it the stream turns/Brambles and grass, to figures in its motion.' Scovell creates a sense of equilibrium that is both precarious and robust, accommodating both 'the fragile water's journey' and the reflection in it of tree and sun, and combining them into 'one continuous substance, each so fixed in flowing.' And just as the evening garden had behind it 'all the universe', so this fragile microcosm and the tiny flowers 'that take the grass/ For cover and the sky, stars in its space' is created by the 'deft and light' touch of time – as far as Scovell is prepared to go, perhaps, towards accepting that creation implies a creator.

Elsewhere, as in 'Unstrained' for example, Scovell is intensely aware that the self-sufficiency of nature is falsified both by the meddlesome imputation to it of some kind of divine pattern and attempts to make sense of its mysteries in art: 'These flowers' beauties were unstrained/...Before my coming laid its human/Abstract intensity upon them/And made a difference I did not intend.' Only the innocence of the child '[un]changed with mortality' who calls flowers 'pretty' not 'beautiful' leaves their featherweight integrity intact:

> 'Pretty' is lighter than a feather
> And moves through flowers like natural weather...
> But 'beautiful' is heavier altogether
> ('Unstrained')

This is an idea to which Scovell returns in the late poem 'The Fish in the Evenlode' in which a 'dark and stubborn fish that stays/Below the stream's engaging surface ways' in water covered by 'white flowers of crowfoot.../

Fairer than if some artist in Japan/Had touched them in faultlessly one by one' becomes a gently understated metaphor for 'the creature's will (unwilled) to be and thrive on earth' at the centre of, and yet completely indifferent to, the artistic composition constructed around it, intent merely on preserving 'its place against the stream'.

If the habit of interrogating nature is a difficult one to break, however, Scovell at least reminds us that it is a habit. In 'African Violets' she goes from asking what it is 'that draws eyes so in these flowers' to wondering what makes us ask such a question in the first place: 'Why should it speak of anything but itself/This little plant merely present.' One answer might be to provide an art that, as she puts it in 'The Geese on the Park Water', is 'constantly flowing/Unless there is God, to waste,' an art that, because she captures it, therefore turns the poet into an almost Cartesian co-witness of creation, an apprehending consciousness that, as she said, was as close as she could get to religious belief. Complete agnostic that she was, however, Scovell's most compelling insights are only visible in certain lights. In 'The Space Between', for example, it is the interstices between the everyday details of the natural world that are made to resonate most suggestively. The organizing principle that can relate flowers seen from a high window 'on the deep-sea garden bed' to layers of cloud – or 'are they foam flecks or mountain waves of sea?' – seen from a plane is conscious enough but the cumulative effect of 'nature's see-through curtaining/Layer upon layer stretched, woven to all degrees/Of part-transparency' suggests an entirely organic natural fabric in which we see through the weft and warp of the world to 'stellar space...the space between.' Art and nature are allowed to speak for themselves and we are left to gaze at the disputed waters between and find God if we want. There are times, of course, when we are reminded how wide these waters are and how much we ask of poetry when we expect it to cross them. In 'The Unwritten Poem'

> The poem will not take its form, will not unravel...
> Knowing its concern is with what hardly can be told,
> Not trusting to this fragile verse
> The marriage and the distances
> Between the seeing mind and the envisioned world
> ('The Unwritten Poem')

The poem here provides not so much a membrane to be permeated as a ligament elastic enough to take the weight of solid objects and propel them into the weightlessness of the imagination, an idea given almost definitive metaphorical shape in 'The Scent':

> She had forgotten, talking, in her hand
> Were roses. Otherwise how could it be
> Their scent had come upon her unawares...
> As happiness can meet one waked from sleep
> And not at first bring back to mind its cause...
> So that bliss hung, before it claimed it was
> Her roses' scent, or had a name at all
> ('The Scent')

The roses' scent – a large part of their 'meaning' – exists almost without reference to their physical existence, a disembodied, nameless bliss, nearly prelapsarian while it lasts but, once it comes into consciousness, carrying echoes, like itself unobtrusive but unmissable, of the Fall.

Appropriately enough, perhaps, for a poet drawn to the mysterious edges of the known, Scovell, like Ridler, writes particularly well about the margins of land and sea. 'Love of the Seashore' is a richly drawn, subtly emblematic poem in which the ebb and flow of the sea, throwing up onto the sand 'the green-veined blue, the oxblood stone', comes to stand for the renewals and redemptions of the 'tidal dailiness of sleep' that 'drown[s] our world to give it back', leaving us with a drift of dreams 'come strange with truth beyond our own/So far-brought, patterned, beautiful'. Ridler's deeply committed Christian outlook – Ronald Gordon recalled that 'nothing could be thought about, or written about, without reference to God'[12] – allows her to find, with Traherne, 'eternity in all appearances' while the agnostic Scovell, more modestly, finds 'all we can bear of infinite' in the sea. But the 'marvels' this brings 'on its flood' are, like her poems, rich and mysterious enough to enchant 'haunters of thresholds', content to stare across them to whatever lies beyond.

Notes

[1] 'Wit and Warmth': Review of 'The Nine Bright Shiners' by Anne Ridler. *Times Literary Supplement* Jan.22, 1944 p.44

[2] 'Cool Confrontations': Review of 'Some Time After' by Anne Ridler. *Times Literary Supplement* Apr.21, 1972 p.441

[3] Obituary of Anne Ridler by Ronald Gordon. *The Independent* Oct.16, 2001

[4] *Collected Poems of Anne Ridler.* Carcanet 2nd ed. 1977

[5] *A Taste For Truth:* A Conversation Between Anne Ridler and Carole Satyamurti, Enitharmon Press 2001 p.31

[6] Obituary of E.J. Scovell by John Mole. *The Independent* Nov.12, 1999

[7] E.J. Scovell in conversation with Jem Poster. *PN Review* 74 16:6 pp.46-48

[8] E.J. Scovell/Jem Poster ibid. [9] E.J. Scovell/Jem Poster ibid. [10] E.J. Scovell/Jem Poster ibid.

[11] *Listening to Collared Doves* by E.J. Scovell. The Mandeville Press 1986

[12] Ronald Gordon ibid.

Peter Dale

The Renunciation of Poetry:
Reflections on Laura Riding's Position

'But truth is like the flight of birds,
Above the head of man.'
— 'Conversation', C. H. Sisson

Mistrust me not, then, if I have begun
Unwontedly and if I seem to shun
Unstrange and much-told ground:
For in peculiar earth alone can I
Construe the word and let the meaning lie
That rarely may be found.
— 'As Well as Any Other', Laura Riding

Several poets, at certain times in their lives, have renounced the pursuit of poetry: Rimbaud, Hopkins, Valéry, to name some of the better known. Of these, only Rimbaud's renunciation was total. He later referred to his poetic endeavours as nonsense or rubbish. Laura (Riding) Jackson's renunciation was noisier and may appear more total in that she took the trouble to state her position forcefully in print. Yet it is less than total, compared with Rimbaud's, in that she allowed both her renunciation and her poems to remain extant, and, indeed, late in life, to be reprinted for a repeat hoo-ha. Despite this, very few poets, critics, aestheticians or philosophers have dealt directly with her case against poetry. Nor can much headway be made here in a brief article but the journey should be attempted. Speaking as a poet, one ought to face the attack that she, a remarkable poet, made on poetry on all fronts.

Put in its most simple — and most complex — form, her case is that poetry fails the truth. It is a statement as plain and, in a different way, as complex as $e = mc^2$ but it has not had the activating effect on the poetry world that Einstein's equation has had on physics. In fact, explanations of relativity theory are easier to follow than some of her exposition of her case.

Both the word 'poetry' and the word 'truth' are terms with fuzzy perimeters if not soft centres when it comes to precise definitions and demarcations. This renders it difficult to see the exact delineation of her case. Yet it is not just the vastness and diffuseness of the view that have led to such caution and hesitation in confronting it. Her explanation of the position also warns people off. The manner of its expression often seems arrogant, vatic, or pontifical;

her prose-style is craggy to little apparent purpose with frequent nonce-phrasing which seems arbitrarily to replace a more readily accessible parlance. Furthermore, her poems not infrequently exhibit a similar diction and are sometimes so extremely abstracted and obtuse that it requires considerable patience with one's own irritation to grasp the intent. Nevertheless, she is on many occasions a remarkably good poet with a quirkily and attractively unique voice in twentieth-century poetry, despite her own view of her poems and poetry in general. She has written enough of such a standard as to demand that her position be faced by any who care for poetry as more than light entertainment.

Yet doubts continue. If poetry's falsity and failure are so fundamental, so widespread, why devote such energy to it or its putative effect? Second, the apparent, or real arrogance, of her style may be misconstrued as a form of megalomania or dottiness; the obscurity of expression may be just that and not the expression of obscurity. On the other hand, this cragginess might be suspected to be a cover, or outer defence-works, for the author's internal doubts about her position, her fear that it is untenable as anything more than a justification for her own endeavours. Finally, history shows quite a number of examples of good poems, one-offs, or two, written by accident or instinct by poets – and some otherwise undistinguished talents or intelligences, literary or otherwise. Her good work may partake of this rather than be the considered, excogitated examples of the deep moral and intellectual inner compulsion to poetry that she claims to have as asserted in her prose and her renunciation.

I am trying to understand her intellectual position here as clearly as possible because of an enthusiasm for many of the poems. This is not made easier by the sense that the 'truth' she seems concerned with is some sort of spirituality, a metaphysical and transcendental truth. She has no apparent doubts as had Pilate. Similarly, her use of the word 'poetry' seems to assume a precise and absolute definition of that term as if poetry had never varied throughout history or throughout a wide variety of cultures. With these uncertainties in mind I'll try to indicate her position by citing, where possible, her own remarks. This brings us to the preface of the 1938 *Collected Poems*.

This preface at first appears to cover some fairly familiar ground. The poet writes from an inner compulsion not always welcomed which 'overcomes a tremendous inertia' ... 'But to describe poetic motivation merely as a compulsion is to conceal a larger part of the story.' She goes on to distinguish two types of compulsion, one external, under which she puts the instigations of the muse of poetry and other external 'divinities' that, in modern times, become 'politics' – this was, of course, written in the Auden thirties era – 'philosophy' or T. S. Eliot's 'tailor's-dummy muse of Religion'. (This is hardly a fair summary of Eliot's rather tortured position. And in terms of truth might seem somewhat ad hominem.) It is probably due to her circumstances in relation to Graves that she sees the muse as an external reality of poetic compulsion rather than as a convenient metaphor for the waywardness of that inner compulsion, a waywardness frequently mentioned by poets of all periods. For her, the only inner compulsion is the poetic one, whatever that may ultimately signify. Poets who act and claim otherwise, in her view, do so to excuse their failures. She identifies a similar inner compulsion in the reader of poetry as the only genuine reason for reading it.

A poem is defined in exalted terms: 'A poem is an uncovering of truth of so fundamental and general a kind that no other name besides poetry is adequate except truth.' ... 'Truth is the result when reality as a whole is uncovered by those faculties which apprehend in terms of entirety, rather than in terms merely of parts.' ... 'A person who writes a poem for the right reasons has felt the need of exercising such faculties, has such faculties.'

As definition these remarks seem by their abstraction and generalness of terms to move rather towards vagueness than precision, fog rather than focus. First there seems to have been made an identity between poetry and truth; the terms seem to her virtually interchangeable. But clearly there are general truths that are not poetry or even verse: 2+2=4 is hardly a poetic statement. 'We all must die' is as true as it gets but it isn't a poem. Nor is it made clear why only general truths should be the essence of poetry. In this generalising she flies in the face of much twentieth-century poetic thought and practice as the term imagism would indicate. Not that such opposition is necessarily misguided but the case for generalisation should have been clarified. Nor is she very forthcoming on what the 'faculties' which will perceive or record these truths in genuine poems consist in or of. Thinkers of the past have named most faculties in fairly clear and approachable ways. Why not use these words to clarify and define the position: faculties of intelligence, imagination, sympathy, empathy, synthesis, the five senses, memory, language?

She finds the writing of the kind of poem she is trying to define an extremely rare occurrence in history: 'But corruption of the reasons of poetry sets in ... when too much emphasis is laid on assisting the reader ... and the poet is more concerned with stirring up the required faculties than with the presenting occasions for exercising them.' This is hardly pellucid. The stirring up of faculties, if done vigorously enough, is likely to exercise them somehow. Without knowing exactly to what human faculties she is referring it is difficult to make a water-tight division between stirring faculties up and involving them in exercise. If, say, imagination is stirred, is it exercised or just a couch potato? However, she rather sweepingly finds that 'The history of poem-writing and poem-reading is in large part a history of such corruption.'

This corruption she summarises in an antithesis of staggering simplification and egocentricity: 'Poets of the English classical period seem giants to us because they were poets by the power of protest.' ... 'So it had to be, more they could not have done.' (But they had attacked falsity – which turns out to be only a negative reason for poetry and thus inadequate: 'poetry positive cannot include the dispute with falsity.' – But presumably her prose can.) Yet it is not clear how the term classical applies to these so-called giants. The romantic figures were 'giant-like in another way.' Having foregone the muscular classical energies and the struggle with falsity, 'Thus disarmed, they were deliberately and hugely weak' ... but 'dreamed hugely of a future in which existence was poetry positive, all of truth.' – How one longs for a name of a poet or poem so that one could get a bearing. Poetry as '*all* of truth' seems an extraordinarily stupid ideal.

The modern period was to synthesise all this. 'These days are, by the laws of temporal and poetic succession, that future in reverence of which the romantics eloquently did nothing.' The word 'laws' here surely would require some definition or proof of existence.

At this point some explanation of the real 'reasons of poetry' seems to be called for but is not going to be forthcoming. Instead we have another staggering assertion: 'But I am not going to give you a list of all the reasons of poetry' ... Instead she proposes to demonstrate the reasons with poems written for all the reasons of poetry – 'poems which are also a record of how, by gradual integration of the reasons of poetry, existence in poetry becomes more real than existence in time – more real because more good, more good because more true.'

She more or less concludes these remarks with a further sweeping recommendation: 'I say, not within the suppositious contexts of religion but within the personally actual contexts of poetry: literally, literally, literally, without gloss, without gloss, without gloss.' If the mind reading a poem doesn't gloss to some extent as it goes it would seem to suggest that the poem it is reading is pre-existent in that mind and reading a mere form of recitation.

It is difficult, also, to see what she means by 'personally actual contexts of poetry' since she regards poems 'that duplicate only the emotions that external objects or scenes inspire – such as wonder, fear, admiration, scorn, tenderness, amusement, and so on' as poems that fail because of an external compulsion rather than an inner. This raises two queries: in this definition are other people merely external objects? This then would lead to a totally solipsistic poetry. Secondly, where does this innerness of the poet come from, if not to some considerable extent from external objects from which this kind of poet is supposedly distinct and isolated? Poets may be born and not made but they are not born with a fully extended human consciousness. Even the pearl has to come from a bit of irritating grit; language and many ideas are acquired from external sources and/or other people.

Difficult it is also to understand her attack on poets who seek to aid their readers when she remarks of herself and her own poems: 'My poems would, indeed, be much more difficult than they have seemed if I did not in *each* [my italics] assume the responsibility of education in the reasons of poetry as well as that of writing a poem.' This would seem to confess of some of her own verse a certain impurity of poetry in her own previously stated terms, indicated above.

The amplification of this preface in the 1980 reprint of her *Collected Poems* seems to throw more confusion than light on her position. She reasserts her exalted view of poetry as 'a tradition of linguistic composition in forms intended for oral or written delivery, of a level of expression above all common levels of expression, and also above the heights of linguistic distinction attainable in learned discourse, philosophic disquisition, the exposition of religious feelings and ideas, the narration of real events or imagined life-experiences for meeting varieties of mentally dignified human interest ...' This talk of levels and heights is in itself metaphorical and doesn't shed much light on the nature of the distinguishing characteristics of these types of expression.

She considers that the modernist movement, however, had effected a degree of change in this exalted field for she continues: 'Until twentieth century literary modernism effected a spiritual alteration in the conception of the nature of poetry, the poetic level of linguistic expression has never been treated as other than of a decreed unique height of linguistic and spiritual distinction ...' (She excepts witty and intelligent light verse and occasions when poetasters have trifled with or neglected the tradition while appearing outwardly to maintain it.)

One problem with this statement about modernism is the phrase 'decreed linguistic and spiritual distinctions' – not to mention how 'unique' is to be taken. It is not easy to see what external 'decree' of these heights Dante, Shakespeare, Wordsworth, Keats, Tennyson, Hopkins or Villon, Baudelaire, Laforgue and Corbière, were obeying, to name a mere handful of disparate poets. One could try dismissing them as some of those who trifled outwardly and negligently with the tradition but if so, which poets carried the veridical tradition across their time to the next generations?

One would like more definition of the spiritual change modernism is supposed to have effected. She puts her own relationship to it but that doesn't clear things up. She assumed the character of a modern in the freedom with which she discarded the 'literary conventionalities' of poetic idiom and made her own poetic diction out of 'natural standards of diction-excellence' and 'shaped it to the requirements of the special concerns of poetry.' This does not seem widely original or divergent from modern poets like Eliot or Pound – at least without some definition of those 'special concerns'. Nor perhaps was her break with the old as consistent as she claims here since her work uses many inversions, some poetic syntax, repetitions, echoes and, on occasion, even 'thee', 'thou' and ''tis'. Hardly current speech even in her day, in Britain or America. It is difficult to see how such minor developments constitute a 'spiritual change' in the nature of poetry.

She claims that poetry 'presents itself as the definition of them [the special concerns of poetry] with the burden of proof put upon the poet of justifying the implicit meaning of the tradition as the union of the highest human concerns within the bounds of poetic expression.' Again we reach the misty heights of some nebulous peak.

She had split this tradition (see above) into two kinds of failure, one classical, one romantic: so how had it previously managed to convey down to her generation these vague 'highest human concerns' that she is apprised of? Poetry presenting the special concerns of poetry is a pretty useless piece of near tautology.

She presents herself as a modernist who had 'not the least difficulty in uniting the traditional character of poetry as an active literature of spirituality with the dignities of modern intellectuality.' – But then linguistic scruples about that endeavour began to surface.

For her, poetry was a pursuit of 'spiritual realism', a fairly tricky concept to grasp in itself, it would seem. Her poems brought her to a position where eventually she 'found poetic utterance arrested even in its being poetic utterance.' She saw poetry as a form of expression limited to 'conventionalities of form that restricted the operation of thought and the rhythmic course of its expression within recitative or song-like patterns.' (This seems, since Coleridge at least, a very narrow view of poetic forms of expression.) But is she saying anything much more than that she did not like current forms in poetry and came to find her own inadequate? (Good reason enough to give up the pursuit without making this song and dance about doing so.)

After so much unsupported and ill-defined assertion, she somewhat petulantly remarks: 'There has been no recognition at all of the unchallengeable logic of my linguistic position, in the time of my working linguistically as a poet...'

The case may rather simply be that her position is so vaguely and abrasively stated that it can barely be grasped – for all her self-asserted claims to pellucid logic.

Her later non-poetic work trying to establish truthful definition of words seems to be as mistaken and misjudged as Casaubon's endeavours with the key to all mythologies. She seems to want to recreate natural language to become other than it is, other than it can be. All one can say is that her endeavours are magnificent in their commitment and energy but Canute-like.

*

Yet since she asserted that the true reasons for poetry are demonstrated or rather contained in her poems perhaps that is where we should now look for clarification. As soon as one turns to them, fine as so many of them are, further hesitations arise. No one would question that they have a characteristic voice, usually a rhythm all her own, and come from an unusual mind and eye on the world. These qualities are to be found in most of the good poets in the tradition she renounced. They cannot then be all that germane in defining her personal inner reasons for renouncing poetic expression – and her poems putatively written for all the real reasons for poetry.

Let's start with a simple example, 'It has been Read by All'. The poem opens by characterising a morning paper's sensational news: a high-speed road-crash, the accident victim a dead child that reappeared before the mother's eyes; a venerable one gone mad in a money-rout; a consumptive daughter of a lord making her own living as a parlour-maid.

The poem proceeds by saying that the public pain distresses the public 'epidermis': the general public feels the tremor as one body whereupon, immediately afterwards:

> The reading heart returns to toast,
> Having fluttered in self-pity
> And felt its best with curiosity.

It is a well enough constructed bit of verse as is normally understood by that; it conveys ideas such as many poets and others have had: that the general public can feel fleeting moments of united feeling; that it generally returns to the immediate concerns of daily actuality shortly afterwards. Nothing of a different kind of truth or deeper attempt at truth is approached than that attempted by many other poets. It is not far from ideas in Auden's 'Musée des Beaux Arts'. In fact, one could imagine a Movement poet like Elizabeth Jennings writing the poem, if a little less craggily.

If one looks at the form, it shows the employment of traditional poetic components – which are not in any obvious way impeding the expression of thought: alliteration; allusion; sound effects; rhythmic devices; lineation and spacing. Yet in her rejection of poetry she claims that such things are a hindrance to thought and truth.

If one remembers that she denied genuine poetry might be written as a response to external stimuli, one might suggest that this poem fails since it springs from a response to a newspaper or a scene in, say, a hotel dining-room. Well, so it might. But any poet, like Riding, who wished to make such a poem, which, as a true poem, she claims, should involve a fundamental and general truth (here, presumably, about human feeling) could well have *imagined* the newspaper and all else in the poem from an inner compulsion, the true source of poems. The real issue is this: whichever the originating stimulus for the poem, how would one stimulus make the resultant poem look different from how it now is – whatever its actual source was? Either stimulus might well end up arriving at this poem.

So wherein lies Riding's overweening claim to the unique specialness of her own poetic endeavour: the poem offers no exceptional deep truth. Its ironic tone was a standard thing in its period and after. Fellow modernists might complain in fact that it is not so well written. It suffers unnecessary inversion in

> and that a child
> Before its mother's eyes a corpse appeared.

It lapses irritatingly in and out of metre. The 'reading heart' seems an authorial skewing of the poem and, possibly, in terms of truth, of the newspaper reader's attitude. Later, the word 'money-rout' draws attention uselessly to its own oddity. The verses do not attempt to be a poem in any more truthful or special way than dozens of poems by other poets that her polemic has condemned. The verses have been criticised here in a way that any other poem might be – which, again, would illustrate its generic likeness as a poem. (Is it perhaps this critical mode itself that is the enemy of the truth she claims to be after?)

If it is objected that this poem is a minor example of the problem she raises, that may well be the case but it was chosen because it shows some of her characteristic quirkiness which one might consider her attempt to shape the truth of poetry she speaks of more precisely 'without gloss' as opposed to other poets' procedures. If one looks at further examples of her work in the collection which she claims to be so much more poetic and truth-seeking and truth-finding than a multitude of other poets' work that she seems to denigrate another quandary arises.

Take for example, the poem from which my epigraph comes. The whole poem has a very persuasive rhythm and content that take a reader in exactly the same way as does any good poem of the tradition that Riding renounces. This suggests that the kinds of truth, the poem-writing and reading-faculties it involves are of the same nature as those of the condemned traditions. Of this poem, Robert Nye wrote, in his Introduction to *A Selection of the Poems of Laura Riding*:

> This ... is prosodically perfect, yet at the same time new and memorable in rhythm, the diction precise, the verbal shape unforced but urgent, the thought and feeling at one and as one truthful.

Clearly, as just remarked earlier, this sort of comment and reaction might be recorded of any number of lyrics in the old traditions she finds so fallacious. Nor does the poem as poem exhibit startlingly new depths or kinds of truth eschewed or traduced by other poets.

If we consider a more quirky poem of hers, one that is well-known and has been often anthologised, 'The Quids', it will serve to demonstrate how skewed Laura Riding's view of her own work had become. Here is a flavour of the poem, the second verse:

> Each quid stirred.
> The united quids
> Waved through a sinuous decision.
> The quids, that had never done anything before
> But be, be, be, be, be –
> The quids resolved to predicate,
> To dissipate themselves in grammar

Riding said, in a recording made in 1972, 'Explaining the Poems', which claimed to correct various confused understandings of the poem:

> Its spirit is not that of philosophical irony. It was an expression of personal dissociation from, rebuff of, the automatic existence processes...

In order to clinch her point she quotes two further verses with which the poem originally concluded in 1924. But if the author needs to re-attach these verses to make clear what she insists her point is, then the poem as collected does not exhibit the qualities she asserts that her collection has demonstrated, as expounded above. In fact, the poem would not necessarily have to avoid 'philosophical irony' to encapsulate her putative meaning for it. Her explanation of it tempts one to say 'I wish she would explain her explanation.'

In his Introduction, just mentioned, Robert Nye avoids this kind of discussion of her renunciation and goes on to remark:

Laura (Riding) Jackson's published post-poetic explanations of her own poems and her reasons for not writing more of them after 1939 leave out of account the involuntary nature of the poetic genius which she undoubtedly possessed.

This seems to be the case. She *is* a good poet. Some of her most striking poems are the lyrics with their quirky memorable rhythms but she also has a vein of sharp irony and satire which is also memorable. She was however no great shakes as a prose-stylist or theorist in prose. Most of her renunciation seems somewhat truculent special pleading. Many poets make mistaken judgements over some of their own works and that of others. Few have been as mistaken as Laura (Riding) Jackson on a whole œuvre.

As for the kinds of truth possible to poetry, that would require more prose and thought than Riding devoted to it. Perhaps Yeats got it about right at least in prose: 'Poetry is truth seen with passion.' But we should add that it is sometimes also passion seen with truth.

The Poems of Laura Riding, a new edition of the 1938 collection, Carcanet New Press, 1980.
A Selection of the Poems of Laura Riding, edited by Robert Nye, Carcanet, 1994.

William Hayward

Six poems and an introductory note

To the Sea

Under the running water there are voices
Sounding where the channel bares its bones;
Behind the weeping eyes the nerves still quiver,
Plucked by a flood of bright fear past those stones.
If you should pan this brain for gold
You'd find a small, hard scream, twenty years old.

Further on the river widens and marshes
Encroach, to still its swift and troubled song;
Fear now is gull-voiced, a bleak, outer crying
Pitched between glut and lust, not right and wrong.
If you should net this mind for fish
You'd catch the skin sloughed off a growing wish.

Sweep in the hungry legions of the sea,
This silt-fouled water stirs their appetite
As human fear most whets the cruelty
Of His fierce love to rive our twitching night.
Now, if you seek to plumb for ground
No echo answers, gone are sight and sound.

(First published *Oxford Poetry 1955* ed. Adrian Mitchell and Richard Selig; Fantasy Press)

The Thaw

His morning walked by roads of ice
Gentled the holy, masking snow
Sun scrutinized the mists, precise
Its questions, airy shapes must go.

No hazard instinct marred the glaze
Where concepts and ambitions spun
Earth could return the sky's clear gaze
Not veiled but armoured from the sun.

Smooth, brittle faith clogged all the rifts
Life ranged a small and hollow sphere
Where soul clogged sense in feet-thick drifts –
Half-seen, another shape drew near.

The silence held, but in the air
Stirred a warm wind. The other's hand
Took strength from his believing stare –
The thaw came, breaking up his land.

Where once was ice, earth holds him bound
Bright clouds have borne away the sky –
My spring of love, now you are found
Ice cannot bind nor fire lick dry.

(1955; Isis Prize Poem, 1956)

Five Birds Rise

Your mind lies open like the map of rivers
Scored in the palm of our accomplished death;
Five birds rise, soaring out of timbered valleys
That guard this world incorporate of our breath;
But when I lie with you
The dusty angels huddle to the ground
And fiery whirlblasts twist the senses round.

Your heart is troubled like the broken water
Of Garple, where it leaves the moors behind,
And pours, dishevelled by high rocks and shingle
Over five holy falls, and then lies blind
Circling and whirled about
In beer-brown pools, where trout savage the flies –
A flick-knife killing, sudden as your eyes.

Your body is a wood where I have built
Five leaky huts to keep my shadows in;
Brown, falling leaves have curtained all the air
And livid colours move beneath the skin,
Proving that I have sown
Some death in you that withers all your grain
While it consumes the substance of my own.

(*New Yorker*, December 1962)

Dusk – Mercombe Wood

This place of beeches is a hermit's mind
Sheer up into the blue dusk his thoughts stand tall
Or stoop within this house, as in a skull
Young voles will cower when the barn-owls call;
Through moonlit columns someone walks away
As if an answer lurked behind the sky.
The killing does not cease by night or day.

No Orphic music can enchant the shapes
That stand about this house, no living mind
Looks out through windows of this tufted skull;
The mirrors have no eyes, the pools are blind;
These beeches clench their fists in the wet clay;
This wood is full of sharp and fearful cries.
The killing does not cease by night or day.

(Broadcast BBC Midland Poets November 1963; published in *The Listener*, October 1963.)

Es Font d'es Marquelle

Water is always a miracle
Cool lip of light tremulous at the stone rim
A massive diamond, containing itself
In itself, like a gap in sound, exploding silently
As green rushes or a tumble of fruiting trees.
When pure, unseen, a true image of the spirit
But quiet-tongued, a Pentecost of whispers
At play with light, deftly, a hand of mirrors
Dealt by a leaping frog or a twitch of insects.
Below us, the sea walks in a skin of silk
A dead tree fingers the sky with exact pointing
But in silent friendship the weather turns green again
New shoots stir in the soil, new words return
Syllables of green and silver, the world made new.

(1966)

Cowper's Winter Walk

When he alone had walked across
The white significance of ground
No foreign print nor outer sound
Betrayed his watching devil in the scene
Only his private loss
Saw white-hot flames beneath that gentle screen

But still the real and fiery sun
Stabbing his back in idle spite
Cast shadows that appalled the light;
His head and all its images must fall
And, growing longer, run
To caper, mocking, on a cottage wall.

(undated, probably 1966)

Introductory Note by Peter Carpenter

William Hayward (September 21st, 1931-December 9th 1968)

William (Curtis) Hayward is probably best known for his correspondence with David Jones, as celebrated in *Agenda* Editions (*Letters to William Hayward* edited by Colin Wilcockson) in 1979. He was also a significant poet, cutting his teeth at Oxford (Merton College) during the early fifties (1952-55) with contemporaries including Elizabeth Jennings, Alan Brownjohn, Geoffrey Hill, John Purkis, Edward Lucie-Smith and Adrian Mitchell. He first met David Jones in 1955 and by 1958 Hayward had visited Jones in Harrow to discuss a proposed commentary on the *Anathemata*; Hayward also met and corresponded with T.S. Eliot over the possibility of publication of the work with Faber. However, a mental collapse in July 1961 stalled this project and others, prefacing, however, much of his most enduring writing in prose and verse over the following three years, including his longest and most ambitious poem, 'The Dance of Earth' and a semi-autobiographical novel, *It Never Gets Dark All Night*, which was published by Heinemann in 1964. This cult novel received very good reviews and Worple Press plans to republish it later this year; a vivid account of the novel and the man can be found in Iain Sinclair's 'London Orbital' (*Granta*, 2002). There are many more fine poems out there and I am thus putting together a *Selected Poems* for publication in 2013.

© Peter Carpenter Literary Editor to the Estate of William Hayward January 2012

Josephine Balmer

A Genuine Art

Nasos Vayenas: *The Perfect Order: Selected Poems 1974-2010*, edited by Richard Berengarten and Paschalis Nikolaou *(*Anvil, 2010).
Alejandra Pizarnik: *Selected Poems*, translated by Cecilia Rossi, (Waterloo Press, 2010).

'In translating poetry,' comments Greek poet Nasos Vayenas in his luminous piece, 'Eight Positions on the Translation of Poetry', 'the original is the experience, and the process of translation is the poetic art.' Certainly every once in a while, a translation of a perhaps previously less known foreign language poet appears in English which not only becomes a modern classic in its own right, but also changes the face of English poetry. For example, Edmund Keeley and Philip Sherrard's translation of C.P. Cavafy's Greek poetry, first published in Britain in 1972, has since become so much a part of both British and American literary culture that it has informed the way in which all subsequent generations have read Cavafy in English, through the filter of Keeley and Sherrard's versions, often as if these *were* Cavafy. In addition, Cavafy's demotic, unadorned style, as well as his trademark poetic historicism and dramatic irony, has proved hugely influential to later English language poets.

The Perfect Order, Richard Berengarten and Paschalis Nikolaou's new edition of Nasos Vayenas, one of the most distinguished of the contemporary Greek poets who can be considered Cavafy's direct heirs, looks set to prove another such classic. Despite the fact that Vayenas is a leading member of the 'Generation of the Seventies' and a winner of the Greek National Poetry Prize in 2005, as well as an esteemed academic, translator and essayist, this is the first full edition of his laconic yet luminous work in English. It includes selections from each of his ten Greek volumes, including his highly-acclaimed 1974 debut collection *Field of Mars*, the innovative *Flyer's Fall* (1989) and *Flyer's Fall II* (1997), in which original poems are interspersed with translations, and 2004's prize-winning *Garland*, his playful faux epitaphs for fictional poets. In addition, a short but extremely welcome selection of Vayenas's critical essays are included, their elegance and clarity highlighting Vayenas's own interest in the work of Ezra Pound and T.S. Eliot.

Most satisfying of all, perhaps, are the poems from Vayenas's mature masterpiece, *On the Isle of the Blest* (2010). This exemplifies his debt to his Greek poetic heritage alongside his connections to a wider European literary tradition. And so his 'Cavafy' is characterised as a chameleon performer:

The multicoloured paper masks you donned
and year in, year out, changed afresh each day,
had wrinkles, ironed their evidence away,
saved you from scorn within your demi-monde.
('Cavafy')

Meanwhile 'George Seferis Among the Statues' foregrounds the ironic intertextuality of Vayenas's work, recalling not only lines of his own Greek mentor (Vayenas's 1979 doctoral thesis was on the elder Greek poet), but also the high modernism of Eliot's Prufrock:

You measured out your life with coffee spoons
looking out over sluggish city rivers
from behind your consulate's grey window
as evening fell upon the green
like a bird with a broken wing.
('George Seferis Among the Statues')

As David Ricks points out in his fascinating introduction, Vayenas is '*par excellence*, a poet-critic', widely-read and hugely discriminating, whose own verse, in its readings of others', as well as in its own precise craft, is always revelatory. Like Vayenas's vision of the iconic Argentinian writer, Jorge Luis Borges, the subject of another poem from *On the Isle of the Blest* (and also another subject of Vayenas's studies, this time for his M.A. in literary translation at the University of Essex), the poet sees through to the soul of his theme:

Living meanings, you plucked things' cores and forms –
leaf-veins, afternoon-hues – light's own strings,
while others caught no more than shades of things.
('Borges')

Such informed – and delicate – textual layers require a very deft hand in their translation. Here Vayenas is wonderfully served by the many distinguished translators whose work is included in the volume, such as David Ricks, Kimon Friar and Roderick Beaton, as well as its editors Richard Berengarten and Paschalis Nikolaou. Together they capture the multiplicity of Vayenas's poetic voices, ensuring that, through their skilful versions, his work, like that of his literary ancestor Cavafy, 'speaks Greek with a slight British accent.'

It will surely not be long before British poets, inspired by this exemplary edition, are returning the compliment.

Across the other side of the world, Borges was also an important figure to his young compatriot, the cult Argentinian poet Alejandra Pizarnik, who died from an overdose of barbiturates in 1972 at the tragically early age of thirty-six; so much so, recounts Cecilia Rossi in her fascinating introduction to Pizarnik's *Selected Poems*, that, on a visit to the elder writer's house with a fellow poet to interview him for a Buenos Aires literary magazine, Pizarnik curled up in an armchair 'like a hypnotised cat', leaving her colleague to ask all their carefully-prepared questions. These days Pizarnik's own eerie and incandescent verse, if little-known in Britain, is capable of inspiring similar reverence, not only in her native Argentina but also in the US where her archive is held at Princeton University. In her short life, Pizarnik was awarded both a Guggenheim Fellowship and a Fulbright Scholarship. From 1960-64 she also lived in Paris where Octavio Paz wrote the prologue for her influential 1962 collection *Diana's Tree*, whose tiny yet succinct poetic pieces seem like fleeting snatches of a lost, parallel world:

> I have taken the leap from myself to dawn.
> I have left my body beside the light
> and have sung the sadness of what is born.
> (*Diana's Tree* '1')

Rossi's new volume includes selections from each of Pizarnik's six main published volumes, from 1956's *Last Innocence* to 1971's *A Musical Hell*, as well as from her uncollected poems, even the lines found on her writing-room chalkboard after her untimely death. Rossi's assured and highly-skilled versions, which have already won awards in both the John Dryden and the Stephen Spender Prizes for translation, now look set to bring Pizarnik's work to a wider audience here in Britain as well, capturing the poems' otherworldliness and mysticism, an enduring sense of how

> the young woman finds the mask of infinity
> and cracks the wall of poetry.
> ('Salvation')

As Rossi notes, citing the influence of Lewis Carroll on Pizarnik's verse, there is a sense of the child's fairy tale about much of this poetry, if more the dangerous, threatening visions of the Brothers Grimm than the reassuring whimsy of Hans Christian Anderson:

> The poem I do not say,
> the one I do not deserve.
> Fear of being two
> the way of a mirror:
> someone asleep inside me
> eats me and drinks me.
> (*Diana's Tree* '14')

Here are the words a figure in a Paula Rego painting might speak, the poems he/she might write; beautiful, disturbing, compelling, the view from the other side of the looking glass:

> You make the silence of lilacs which shake
> in the tragedy of the wind of my heart.
> You made of my life a children's story
> where shipwrecks and deaths
> are excuses for adorable ceremonies.
> ('Acknowledgement')

Working on such brief pieces is far more difficult that it might at first appear, calling for the sureness and accuracy of a surgeon's hand. 'What does it mean to translate oneself into words?' asks Pizarnik in 'The Cure of Folly'. As her introduction reveals, Rossi has clearly spent a great deal of careful thought and study on answering such a question, citing, as example, her six drafts of a single line from Pizarnik's enigmatic uncollected poem 'Of Silence'. Rossi's meticulous approach is well worth the effort as she settles on her final, suitably gnomic form: 'I was the impossible and also riven by the impossible.'

For Nasos Vayenas, in Paschalis Nikolaou's crystal-clear English version of 'Eight Positions on the Translation of Poetry', 'if the translation of poetry is impossible, then the translation of poetry is a genuine art.' These two important new volumes, both set to become modern translation classics, are proof of such art at the highest level. As Vayenas's own 'Cavafy' concludes:

> Your word lays bare the ways
> that the soul is what a poem's lines reveal...
> ('Cavafy')

Peter Dale

Labradorescence

A fragment of labradorite, purchased where?
A comfortable handful or piece to display,
palm-size the edges natural, face polished smooth.
In changing lights of day and night it gives:
a small bay, cliff enclosed, its scythe of sand,
over-arched by wind-warped saplings, larger boughs;
or creek, moon-bright; the lateral flame of a stream;
or tide of amber sunrise – all from cliff height.

Places we've seen? Or does it inculcate
scenes where neither it nor we have been?
In other hands and angles, different sights?
Our haven, cliff – one day we'll find the place
– or, unaware, project it on some likely bay
with this uncanny sense of déjà vu.

Robert Wells

Ionian

O estuaries, anchorages

    that bay
where the fresh meeting the salt water
ran cold above it,
and the swimmer there
churning the levels together
started with his movement
– by some chemistry –
a precipitate,
clouding about his limbs.

O harbours, hinterlands

    a broken
sarcophagus on the foreshore;
a line of arches, weatherworn,
striding with vain purpose
into the wood
– too easily whetted
a taste for elegy,
the greeds and cruelties
long gone elsewhere.

O ragged coasts, rough capes

    the boat riding
offshore where no beach opened
– heave of water
against the abrupt stone,
a pine grove where cicadas
scratched their song so loud
by hot mid-morning
that the sound came
distinct across the surge.

O fellow-travelling creatures

    dolphins
within the prow's torn backwash
rising alongside,
embodiments of the wave
– suddenly outside it
and ahead in varied play,
the propulsion without visible cause;

so, stationary-seeming
as if stamped in silver.

   O evidences of passage

    ruts in rock,
a coin, a figurine,
potsherd litter, an amulet
pulled from riverbank gravel
– less these leavings
than the journey retrieved and known,
sea true to its old epithets,
day measured by the sun
lifting and sinking.

Robert Hamberger

Being the Sea

This morning
gulls float on my skin like a hand
across a forehead, the skim of it
feeling my chill, my fever.

One wave cuffs another like heartbeats,
my eardrum pulsing whenever I dream.
Fish swerve through me in glittery shoals,
the nets half-empty on a late afternoon
although a shark still hangs by my quayside,
the suede of its fin stroking my finger.

My edge casts a handful of pebbles
an inch from your ankle.
My tide shoves rocky heaves
hard against crashed weather.
Hours sway past turquoise to gun-metal,
flamingo to peach when the sun gives up.

Scrunch your heels beside my ebb.
Listen tonight at last for my hiss:
it's nearly a promise, almost a threat
in the moon's white dazzle over black shallows,
my cloak of oceans, my marvellous deep.

Clare Best

How they are at home

He's never been the sort of man to note
the length of her skirt, or how she hums
when she sets the breakfast out
before they go to bed. Instead
he stares across the pond, seeing
black on the surface. And he notices the lawn:
how green, how very green it is.
He doesn't seem to hear
the way her voice slides upward, saying
Tomorrow? as he puts his lips to hers.

At first she's sad he won't admire
her slender legs. But then she gives away
the shorter skirts, listens to silence
as she sets the breakfast out.
She stocks the pond with carp, to interest him.
He's busy, seeing black. She wonders
if he'd like a dog, another home,
a better lawn. More green.
He says, *Just this – I want to kiss you,*
hear you say 'Tomorrow' like you always did.

How she walks home

She looks in, where windows lack curtains or blinds.
Number Five, mute emulsion and gilt-framed portraits, spotlit –
a set where the actors have not yet appeared.
Number Nine, half-dark upstairs – two bodies embrace against red.

Now only yards away – the chimney stencilled on a wash of sky,
stairwell glowing, curtains swagged to the side. She imagines
the slew of post behind the door, in the kitchen
a pulsing answerphone. Him, in his usual chair.

But this time she walks on, as if the place was never hers –
and she climbs the narrow lane, into the night
where hedge shelters fox and shrew,
the only light the scattered tinsel of stars.

Matthew Barton

Fall Snow

Fall snow and cover all the hurt we've done
to one another. Overlay the ache
of lovelessness with your oblivion.

You kiss me with forgiveness, make loss one
single dress of silence, flake by flake:
fall snow and cover all the hurt we've done

with soft resolve. There's nothing that you shun,
so kneel down from the night and gently wake
our lovelessness into oblivion.

We can't relent. And soon we will be gone.
But soothe us snow, erase our harsh mistake:
fall snow and cover all the hurt we've done,

and bless us now despite ourselves. Though none
but we can make amends, your whisperings speak
all lovelessness into oblivion.

Cover our traces as we stumble on:
fill up our tracks, keep tumbling full and thick –
fall snow and cover all the hurt we've done,
spread over lovelessness oblivion.

Jane Lovell

Snowy Egret

You think 'white'.
You think 'sword of a beak'.

You see curled vinyl feet, bleached and flayed by wind
and tide, tight-clenched on evening air,
the last dregs of light.

A loosened feather bellying the river lifts and floats and falls,
rides the water.

Inside the carcass: a perished stomach, remnants of its final meal.
Bones of fry flare from tiny vertebrae, buckled spines;
pinchbone skulls brittle in a vault of ribs:
flittering life held an instant in the sly lens, flipped and
speared and twisting.

What colour, survival?
Blackest eyegleam, chiselled water;
white of feather, sky and bone.

What shape?
It curves. It sweeps and circles, lands.
A crescent, looping, sealing its descent with a tight
knot.

You travel the cello-curve of pelvis, trace brim and spine of ilium;
contemplate the skull that twists and turns and sinks its chin upon its chest
to pass;
and your own, small, unborn life,
your own, small, unborn life, bone within bone tangled;
the snag of legs.

Life is built on bolts of chance.

Released, this tiny life now grown, beside you walks,
comments on the darkening sky,
the egret black-eyed in the dusk.

It takes your breath, the tattered beauty of the resolute,
this hunter hunched about its heartpulse,
frozen outwards from the barest flicker of its eye.

Penelope Shuttle

Single

There's not enough music for one song,
not enough light for one last day.

There's not enough sleep for one dream,
enough tears for a single grief,
enough words to make amends.

There's not enough truth to mend one lie,
nor enough thorns for one rose,

and never enough linen for a shroud,
no matter how often you fold and measure,
never enough veils for Salome to shed,
dancing and stripping at her leisure.

Sleeping-in

Sleeping-in
after journeying,

then waking to an empty house
and *Time that moves in circles*

April's done and dusted,
says Time,
May's green and white drama begins

Fair enough, mon ami

But then Time rings
the lark's song
from years ago in my ears,

you and I stand amazed by life
on Goonhilly's rough golden heath

long ago

and now I don't know which way to turn
out of this circle of song I'm life-lost in

William Oxley

Old Gate of Essex

Years ago I wrote of you, and now
I think of you again, old gate of Essex
over which time has crawled slower than moss
or maybe not at all. Ash keys helicoptered
down around me and small twigs broke off
the lion-bodied oak in a wind from
the white distance beyond your spars
and cross-patternings of rain-ribbed wood.
Field gate to a world forgotten
in the scientific fantasy and frenzy in which we live!
You were a pattern nailed on air,
a brief geometry of wood.
I leaned on you, touched your porous planks,
knew you a barrier to flower-muddled meadows
and private parks of silence, a gate
that symbolized in humble commonsensical way
the glimpsed but unreachable meaning
of a landscape that cannot be trespassed.

Will Stone

Le Château de Valgenceuse

A memory of the Valois

Lost domain, happy fault in the loom,
miracle borne on the dark conveyor of our time,
gift given only when death's back is turned.
You enter and are the only one to breathe
the heavily misted avenues of yew,
soil fragrant urns and perfectly weighted pools.
Ferns, their juvenile green forcing speech
from unworldly grey stone, naiads' voices
smoked out by the Nonette's slow turns.
On the lake's slender arm, two black dragon flies
repair the nets of surface shadow,
a plash and a plop, the otter's frozen muscle.
Our eyes are one, just for a moment
then mine are left, toys abandoned,
the surface suddenly remade, never broken.
Between the anchor roots of the island
and over slippery hooped bridges of iron
to the giant shell of the summerhouse,
where poets stooped in mossy silence
and now a grey fox springs, nailed to a board
unblinking for eternity, his escape preserved.
But new visitors are dismantling the dream,
each holds a piece and one by one they come
as if requested to endorse your draining away,
as you return over lawns tenderly furred by sun.
At the gates a concealed Lord abruptly looms…
'Monsieur, c'est vous qui avez traduit
notre grand poète Gérard de Nerval?'
Yes sir and I believe he once took from here
the four huge letters that make up *hope*,
until beside the Acheron they laid him out.

Sue Roe

Dream of a Dress

having nothing to open the large box
which had for a long time been silent
I took a backless dress of starkest crimson
used it as a key

sculpted quite fortuitously to fit the lock
it started up the music of the piano
sounds of quick, staccato, clockwork notes
to rhythms set by hammers and a handle

dolls in rows were dancing on their shelves
rocking horses rocking with no riders
the attic set in motion in the small hours
a sudden, sputtering magic lantern show

I watched it through the doorway in my dress
then stole away and wore it in the streets
it had a dual purpose, haunting people
and warning them not to touch

it gave me a secret entry
I used it to watch the night through

Radial Space

her face slips through
slides beneath the surface
he knows he can't secure her
paints to remind himself

she's a mental trampolinist
tight-rope walker, acrobat
and he is only one clown,
auguste, her old accomplice

their words echo to silence
a violin in a collage
paper and broken strings
empty of music

after the ball
he sits her on the broken chair
paints her in blatant green
her fan partially unfolded

she looks at the picture
objects to his *rapports*
her face, thighs, her expression
vacant, variegated

a study in composition
and she, wedged in a triangle,
a complementary carving
but she can't see what she's complementing

Robin Renwick

If

If, my darling,
I could take all the sadnesses
that you have ever known, that are
turning to stone within you still,
and hold them in my cupped palm,
I'd make of them a white dove
all feathered with soft caresses
and let it loose on the green hill
for the world's winds to carry.

And, my love,
if I could take your every smile
and keep it in a precious jar
then, once in a while, I would try
to ease away the sorrow from your soul
and use your own sweet balm
to show you who you are.

The Ram

Later in life I discovered how it worked,
a simple pump, driven by the flow
of a small stream, needing no power
and little maintenance.

        All that we knew
was that it was yellow, and it had
a black swastika emblazoned on its side.
And it ticked, a slow relentless sound
that never faltered.

        The danger was clear.
We kept our distance, dared each other
to get closer, included it in our games,
hurling grenades of clay from the long grass
and the dead ground.

        We learned to live with it.
And something has remained over the years,
part of our world, drifting into dreams,
touching us, like a light breeze from childhood days
that carries the sound of bells, a distant siren.

John Gladwell

Measuring Each Angle

Measuring each angle
Drawing a new diagram and then describing analysing each number

Predetermining each level
Then trying to describe what it is a surface unsatisfactory

So cling carefully
Attach yourself to waiting to observing a new treatment

A new climate of change
To congregate to create heat cognition

Driving the past home
Towards this place of almost disbelief

Where you call out my name
Your diaphragm moving no exit no memory

Just a blind echo immortalised by slow degrees
Expecting no comfort no proof just each day's survival

In the abeyance of an ancient law
With nothing now left to subtract except coincidence

No justice no blind chance
Just the open wound of your absence

A cold wind for August midday
And the moon's negative still hanging low in the sky.

Mandy Pannett

Begin with a riddle

Begin with a riddle, my lord would say,
those winter nights when I was his bard
and the mead-hall rang with my song:

> *A harbinger of early spring*
> *sometimes heard but seldom seen*
> *I sing my name.*

> *Abandoned by my closest kin*
> *I bear the blast of others' scorn*
> *the lightning-lash of rain.*

Now spear-men trap me in this fen
where flies with fretful-weary wings
lurk in a marsh-mire gloom.

They are liars, those who call me
outlaw, wolf's-get, thief –

They would kill my best of dreams,
fell me at the forest's edge,
allow the sea to sip my bone,
clod me in dark earth.

I would have a sester of honey,
snout of a plough to furrow my land,
the fins of an anchor to hold me steady
in the dash and dazzle of waves.

Wait, my girl with plaited hair,
wait at dawn by Cyrtlan gate,
the deer pool next to Tuha's tree,
wait three days for me.

The *cuckoo* is the bird of spring
who cries his name in double notes
and warms his frost-breath winter quills
with candles of the sun ...

Now let Spring,
that laughter-smith, bind
the eagle's claws in blossom,
fill a basket with blue sky and tip it
down through heaven's leaves to drench
my roots, to sing, to bring me home.

D.V. Cooke

The Dance of Death

Take these words and nascent be
Staggered by eternity.
Among the labyrinth of your tears
Time may wander lost for years.
Language loves you but will it last
Where music begins its vast
Seraphic sound of angel wings
That moves the air then louder sings.

Our uncooked lives should appeal
And of these graves make a meal,
Or send for honey or a hive,
And thirst for fish that yet thrive
A mile below an English sea –
All to be found in poetry
That waits four centuries until
Tombs and emperies have their fill.

Where worms devour the human heart
Yet leave these bones as an art,
Laid out in stone and symmetry
Of what was you and once was me,
Where now – if you do so please,
Congregations of drowsing bees
Hum hymns and dunces in their dance
Build monuments to indolence.

While in a stone mausoleum
Music moves a terse *Te Deum*,
As Helen – dressed for some new Troy,
Returns disguised as a boy.
Fashion and politics here lie
In one unconvivial sty –
Where *Dullness* descends the stair,
A pig's tail woven in his hair.

Here the grave melts down its guest
And makes a meal out of a jest –
Which brings the war-drum roll and dance
Of death's dark rattling cadence.
Sweet and low the voices soar
To drown and down the dance of war,
Until night brings showers of rain
As each is if made one again.

Phil Cohen

Carrying the Torch? Poetry, Sport and the Cultural Olympiad

Poetry seems to be very much in place for the London 2012 Olympics. The Cultural Olympiad features Poetry Parnassus, a five-day festival to 'celebrate language, diversity and global togetherness', with one poet from each of the 205 competing nations reading from their work, which is to be published as a 'World Record' of the multicultural event. In contrast the 'Winning Words' project is creating a series of local, site-specific, 'poetry installations' in the Olympic Park. Lemn Sissay's poem 'Spark catchers', for example, is written on a wooden fence surrounding an electricity generator. It seems strange, given this mode of visual display that a typographical or 'concrete' poem was not commissioned. Still you can't have everything and Jo Shapcott has been commissioned to write a poem on swimming, John Burnside on cycling, while Carol Anne Duffy tries her hand at paralympic tennis.

It is not all good news. The project also invited the public to nominate their favourite poems as a source of inspiration for the Olympic athletes. The BBC sports broadcaster John Inverdale, one of the panel of judges, suggested 'The Victor' by C. W. Longenecker as an example of the kind of thing they were looking for. The poem includes the verse:

> If you think you'll lose, you're lost.
> For out in the world we find
> Success begins with a fellow's will.
> It's all in the state of mind.

which is almost as bad as Jeffrey Archer's nomination from 'The Ladder of St. Augustine' by Longfellow:

> The heights by great men reached and kept
> Were not attained by sudden flight,
> But they, while their companions slept,
> Were toiling upward in the night.

The winner, Tennyson's 'Ulysses,' put a similar sentiment much more concisely and as a result has had its lines 'to strive, to seek, to find, and not to yield' suitably inscribed on a memorial at the centre of the Olympic Village. Meanwhile up and down the country, poetry competitions have been staged, taking the Olympics as their theme. The Greater London Authority organised a competition on '100 things I like about the Olympics', while the *Guardian* commissioned poems from some of our leading practitioners on sporting and Olympic themes.

All this activity raises some interesting questions about the status of poetry within our public culture, and also its relationship to sport.

As a domain within the republic of letters Poetry is an appropriately 'auto-poetic' activity. It has its own institutions, its diverse schools and cultural traditions, its hierarchies of esteem, its rituals of peer recognition. As a community of practice it is both self organising and largely self referential. Poets learn their craft by reading other poets, and nowadays by attending creative writing courses taught by them. In the typical public reading, the audience is almost entirely made up of other poets, whether amateur or professional. Yet Poetry has always had its wider arenas, occasions when it emerges from the literary margins and takes centre stage in the nation's cultural life. Sometimes – rarely – this occurs spontaneously. The death of Lady Diana was probably the last time this happened in Britain when professional poets joined thousands of amateurs up and down the country in writing verse to express their sorrow. More usually, of course, it is a matter of commission from some public body or branch of government.

Poetry is supposed to be memorable speech, so it not surprising that poets should be called upon when some important event or circumstance has to be officially celebrated or memorialised. Until quite recently the Poet Laureate had a virtual monopoly on the job, not that having to write verse to commemorate the Queen's Coronation and birthday, the births, marriages and deaths of other members of the Royal household, visits from heads of state or other dignitaries and famous victories in war was regarded by most of the post holders as more than an irksome task.

Today the practice of commissioning poems to mark some special event has widened considerably in scope as the calendar of official celebration and commemoration has enlarged, and many more poets get the call. The bi-centenary of the founding of the Post Office, the 150th anniversary of the publication of Darwin's *Origin of the Species,* the 50th anniversary of the ending of the Second World war, have all been occasions for the commissioning of important work on these themes. Now there are suggestions that poems might be commissioned in connection with special weeks or days designed to publicise and raise money for Good Causes: Famine Relief, War on Want.

And then, of course, in more celebratory mode, there is the Olympics. Mark O'Connor, the Sydney Olympics Laureate, got paid 80,000 dollars for penning the following unforgettably regrettable lines :

Never has so much jog and slog
gone into maintaining a metaphor.
something you pass on, don't keep for long,
but make sure someone else has got it, sort of.

If William McGonagall had got to translate Pindar's 'Ode to Asopichus,' the result would surely be better than this!

If commissioned poetry, verse 'made to order', has a bad reputation amongst the poetry community, this is mainly because, with a few honourable exceptions, so much of it has been so bad. The desire to find 'memorable speech' has resulted in distinctly unmemorable verse. Who can remember a line of the poem commissioned to mark the inauguration of President Obama?

Part of the suspicion about commissioned work is the widely held belief that the occasions of poetry should be spontaneous, not contrived, freely chosen, not commanded. There is an element of bad faith in this. Many poetry competitions dictate topic, verse form and even length, and poets enter them in great numbers for the sake of the challenge they represent. But there are also justified fears that extending the practice of commissioning could lead to poetry becoming just another arm of the advertising industry or political spin machine. Poets embedded by the Ministry of Defence with our troops in Afghanistan may no longer have to face direct censorship in what they write, but they are under more subtle pressures to shift their angle of vision to that of a British soldier looking down a gun sight at 'the enemy'. It is difficult to see how poems commissioned to launch a new line of beauty treatments, open a corporate HQ or publicise a casino, not to mention poems featuring 'product placement', could be said to be advancing the cause of putting truth back into words.

The occasions of poetry
The strenuous attempt to reinstate poetry in the public sphere has to be seen against the background of its atrophy in popular culture and private life.[1] In the 1950s, my dad used to come into my bedroom every morning at about 7 am, fling the curtains wide and declaim the opening lines of Edward Fitzgerald's translation of the *Rubaiyat of Omar Khayyam:*

AWAKE ! For morning in the bowl of night
Has flung the stone that puts the stars to flight
And lo! The hunter of the east has caught
The sultan's turret in a noose of light

His intention was to instil in me his own love of poetry (he could quote large chunks of Shakespeare and was never without a quote from Burns to suit almost any family occasion). And no doubt he hoped that these wonderful words would sugar the pill of having to get out of bed on a cold winter's morning and go to school. But somehow the attempt to kill these two birds with a single poetic stone didn't quite work. If my already well developed dislike of school got transferred to poetry, it was because one of the more exquisite tortures inflicted on us as ten and eleven year old prep school boys was having to memorise quite long poems by Wordsworth, Shelley, Byron, Longfellow and Tennyson for our homework, and then get up and recite them in front of the whole class. You can imagine the delight when one of us faltered, got a word wrong, or just dried up. Not to mention what the boys with speech impediments went through, for they were not spared this exercise in collective sadism.

No doubt the whole thing was designed more as an exercise in public speaking and memory building than poetry appreciation, and the fact that it had such a negative effect on so many of us is probably to do with the school's peculiar ethos. Perhaps it was also a throwback to a time when poetry had more of a walk-on part in the culture of the English educated elite – the ability to turn out a half decent sonnet, translate Tennyson into Greek iambic hexameters, or introduce an appropriate quotation from Shakespeare, Milton or Keats into the conversation being an important part of a young gentleman's social equipment.

Yet it is important to remember that in 18th and 19th century Britain the capacity to recite or quote quite long passages of verse was a quite widely disseminated skill in both town and countryside. In Elisabeth Gaskell's novel, *Cranford*, a yeoman farmer is described as having his cottage crammed with books of verse, and quoting at length from them as he walked his woods. Artisans could also quote chapter and verse, and not only from the Bible. In a more secular age, with the arrival of first the music hall and then steam radio, the recitation of light verse in the form of comic or dramatic monologues was a regular feature of the bill. Stanley Holloway did the rounds with his famous rendition of Albert and the Lion and would have the audience reciting along with him as he tells the cautionary tale of Mr and Mrs Ramsbottom's visit to the zoo in Blackpool and their son's unfortunate encounter with a lion called Wallace.

Today the ability to quote, let alone recite whole poems, is increasingly confined to graduates of English departments and professional poets – and quite a few of them have a surprising inability to remember any poems other than their own. The idea that poetry should be part of every well-stocked mind does, of course, survive; it is a continual refrain of poetry's public evangelists.

For example the Poetry Aloud group recently launched a national recitation project in an attempt to revive the practice. But if such initiatives seem to be falling on so many deaf ears, it is largely because they are listening – and chanting aloud – to the deafening lyrics of pop songs or rap. Moreover the internet offers an instant collective memory with sites listing quotations from poets on any subject under the sun, ready to be cut and pasted into your latest essay or talk.

Poetry is, by definition, the enemy of kitsch. In *The Incredible Lightness of Being* (1974), Milan Kundera defined kitsch as 'whatever denies or excludes the negative aspects of life and satisfies the need to gaze into the mirror of the beautifying lie and be moved to tears of gratification at one's own reflection.' The 2012 Olympics, with its invocation to 'live the dream' and insistence that 'everyone is a winner' is full of kitsch – just look at its mascots and the proposed 'Isle of Wonders' scenario for the Opening Ceremony[2] – and that is why poetic engagement with it is both necessary, important and problematic. The difficulty of the challenge is illustrated by the poetry installation project. The poems had to be short, 'punchy' and accessible, as well as specific to the Olympic site and this brief inevitably limited the field to poets who can work in a condensed and popular idiom. 'Winning Words' not only echoes the London 2012 strap line but suggests something both aspirational and beguiling. This might be a good enough description of advertising copy, but as a definition of poetry's mode of address it leaves a lot to be desired.

Beyond the two cultures
2012 offers an unparalleled opportunity to bring the worlds of poetry and sport into closer conversation with one another. It may well be the case that European poetry came into existence with the Olympics and Pindar's odes in praise of its athletes, but in modern times they have existed on different planets. C.P. Snow talked about the two cultures of the humanities and sciences, but the arts and sports have also gone their separate ways. Brain and Brawn, Bohemian and Body Builder, Aesthete and Athlete, Wimp and Jock, until very recently, these binaries and the stereotypes they underwote, prevailed.

The historical association of athleticism with muscular Christianity, and of organised team games with the Public school ethos, the values of Nation and Empire, summed up in Sir Henry Newbolt's 'Vitai Lampada' ('Play up! play up! and play the game!') for a long time made their rejection almost mandatory for left wing intellectuals and budding artists. Yet those committed to the life of the mind often secretly admired, and even envied, those who pursued the life of the body. Some of the Bloomsberries were keen supporters of the 'noble art' and used to make surreptitious trips to the East End to watch their heroes in action in the ring. The reinvention of the Olympics by Baron de Coubertin as a modern day version of the 'Hellenic Ideal' provided a rationale for many an erstwhile 'weed', educated in the Classics, to come out of the closet and declare their passion for sport. In the 1930s Henri de Montherlant wrote a lyrical evocation of Olympic athleticism[4] which scarcely concealed the nature of its desire, although his example was not followed in the more cloistered world of English letters, except for John Betjeman's 'Ode to a Subaltern' with its mischievous lines : 'What strenuous singles we played after tea, / We in the tournament – you against me! // Love-thirty, love-forty, oh! weakness of joy / The speed of a swallow, the grace of a boy.'

In his autobiography *Tennis Whites and Teacakes* Betjeman records the division between 'hearties' and 'arties' in the Cambridge of the inter-war years, but despite, or perhaps because of, variously transgressive forays across the Great Divide, it persisted well into the post-war period. Wendy Cope, writing about 'Sporty people', records the sense of shock that accompanied her friendship with a Junior County tennis champion:

How could it happen?

She wasn't stupid. She read books.
She had never been mean to me
For being bad at games.
I decided to forgive
Her unfortunate past.

Given that sport and poetry have occupied such different universes of discourse, it is not surprising that those who are good at pentameters and those who shine in the pentathlon don't often find much common ground. Sometimes they have admired each other from a distance, or ventured into each other's territory while still keeping the two worlds separate. A.J Ayer was a keen Spurs supporter and James Joyce loved – and played – cricket but I doubt anyone would see this as key to understanding logical positivism or *Finnegans Wake*. Camus played in goal for Algiers but the *Myth of Sisyphus* is not usually interpreted as being about his team's struggle for promotion to the first division. Equally, when asked about their performance, few modern sprinters are likely to reply: 'Well, John, I think reading Derrida during training really helped me get my head in the right space, and gave me the edge coming off the bend'. But they may, nevertheless, be studying for an Open University degree in Social Science.

So some of the stereotypes have begun to crumble. Sport, for intellectuals and artists, is no longer the love that dare not speak its name. It is routine for academics in search of street cred to boast of their devotion to the beautiful (and once upon a time the People's) game. There is a whole research industry devoted to the study of every aspect of sport. Poets play football and cricket, and a few even write about it. You can go to Loughborough University and get a degree in Sports Psychology whilst continuing to train for the Olympics. All appearances to the contrary, Mike Horovitz, daddy of the English beat poets, and presiding genius of the 'Poetry Olympics' is by his own account a dedicated 'Midsummer Morning Jogger' as well as a keen follower of Wolverhampton Wanderers FC – the title of his epic poem about Britannia. Horovitz was a pioneer in this as much else, but today the baton has been handed on. Poetry slammers with their high energy verbal athleticism are closer to bridging the gap, as, from the other side of the tracks, are those Olympic sports like gymnastics, ice skating, and synchronised swimming where the aesthetic dimension, the gracefulness displayed, is as important as technique in judging the performance.

This raises the thorny issue of the relation between poetry and sport as forms of aesthetic experience. They perhaps have more in common than is often recognised. The iambic, which is still the pulse of so much English verse, is only a heartbeat away from the poetics of athletic endeavour. In his 'projective' approach to poetry, Charles Olson wanted to literally breathe life back into verse by making it dance not to metre, but to a more embodied rhythm as in his famous dictum 'the HEAD, by way of the EAR, to the SYLLABLE / the HEART, by way of the BREATH, to the LINE.'

Similarly many accounts by athletes of being 'in the zone' of peak performance, where they feel 'lost in focused intensity', approximate closely to the states of mind recorded by artists and writers when they are at work and which can also be summoned up when reading poetry or listening to music. In his book *In Praise of Athletic Beauty* (2006) Hans Gumbrecht has made a cogent plea for recognising sport, both in its performance and spectatorship, as a primarily aesthetic experience. He chides academics for feeling obliged to interpret sports as expressive of wider – and usually negative-social forces, rather than understanding them in their own terms for the forms of excitement, pleasure, and entertainment they yield.

Gumbrecht's phenomenology of playing and watching sport certainly does articulate much that is normally ignored or taken for granted by sports writers, fans and athletes themselves. Nevertheless it is as if there is something about the visceral aesthetics of sport which makes it difficult for both participants and spectators to translate into words and images that do justice to its complexity and emotional depth. Sports writing at its best captures some of the momentary excitements, but the deeper structures of feeling escape it, and we are mostly left with the tired clichés of triumphalism. This is where poets come in. The moves and the balletic agility of footballers, the timing and elegant stroke play of true batsmanship (as opposed to 20/20 slogging) in cricket, are surely worthy subjects for lyric. Cricket, at least, for so long a pastoral metaphor the English lived by, has inspired poetic appreciation: Wordsworth, Tennyson, Betjeman, Housman and Ted Hughes being of the number, while, today, Kit Wright has reinvented the game as a way writing more reflexively about what its heritage now represents[5].

Winning Words? Poetry goes on location
A sense of heritage was also central to the Olympic Park commissions. All the chosen poets have been concerned to dig beneath the scrubbed surface of the Park, and like true archaeologists they have found buried treasures amidst what to other eyes is just another heavily polluted brownfield site. Each poem takes us on a journey across a narrative landscape where traces of this otherwise hidden history and geography emerge, at times surprisingly. Jo Shapcott's 'Wild Swimmer', perhaps inspired by Roger Deakin's *Waterlog*, heads off across country and discovers a whole network of 'lost' rivers, canals and waterworks. Some of it is tough going: 'all swamp/and sewage until the Northern Outfall drain', but the wild swimmer is enjoined to persist and 'backstroke through the past/and remember how Alfred the Great/dug the Channelsea to keep out Danes'. So some of the familiar features of our 'island story' surface albeit in unlikely places. Unlike Roger Deakin's book, the poem does not explore the sensuous delights of swimming and turns into a bit of a travelogue : 'Count off rivers as you swim: Bow Creek, the Waterworks/the Channelsea, the City Mill, Hennikers Ditch'; it ends up, predictably enough, back in the Aquatics Centre, where, mindful of her commission, Jo Shapcott urges her swimmer to 'swim your heart out, for you are all gold.' Such 'winning words' sum up the poem's rather winsome quality.

'Wild Swimmer' invites comparison with U.A. Fanthorpe' s famous poem about London's lost rivers, but 'Rising Damp' occupies a much darker, more troubled terrain. Her rivers are 'disfigured, frayed, effaced':

They have gone under.
Boxed, like the magician's assistant.
Buried alive in earth.
Forgotten, like the dead.

Fanthorpe's waterways are spectral presences that continue to haunt the city, they 'infiltrate chronic bronchitis statistics', and 'will deluge cellars, detonate manholes/plant effluent on our faces,/sink the city.'

There is no way such an apocalyptic vision could have been allowed to contaminate the clean green environment that is Olympic Park and Jo Shapcott steers well clear of exploring the darker underside of her poetic landscape. In contrast Lemn Sissay's poem was inspired by the 'danger of death' signs that are fixed to electricity transformer enclosures; this lethal aspect of 'sparks flying' led him to the old Bryant and May factory on the edge of the Park, where in 1888 Annie Besant organised a famous strike of the 'match girls.' Never mind its somewhat obvious word play as the different meanings of strike are permutated, 'Spark Catchers' is a poem with attitude; with its jagged rhythms and angry assonances, its 'sulphurous spite filled spit', it is made to be performed, chanted, or shouted aloud. Despite its incantatory style the poem has its odd lyrical moment: 'Beneath stars by the bending bridge of Bow/In the silver sheen of a phosphorous moon/They practised Spark Catching.' But the dominant mood, and diction is militant and 'in your face' quoting words from Besant's article on 'White Slavery in London': *"The fist the earth the spark its core/The fist the body the spark it's heart"*/The Matchmakers march. Strike.'

John Burnside's poem, 'Bicycling for Ladies' takes its inspiration from another famous socialist and feminist, Sylvia Pankhurst, who worked in Bow for some years and was a keen cyclist. There are two sections, each with epigraphs which point to his sources; these include sayings from some of the working class women who collaborated with Pankhurst, Yardley advertising material and an early text on women's emancipation through cycling which gives the poem its title. From this disparate set of co-ordinates Burnside conjures up a multi-layered landscape which moves effortlessly between the personal and political dimensions of its subject. He portrays the aspirations of the cyclists in terms of a social geography which lays claim to a national heritage from which they have historically been excluded:

not for them the solitude of some
far crossroads, with its litany of names
from ancient times,

they want to ride for hours, on country lanes
through Saxon woods and miles of ripening grain
and end up at some point of no return,

like changelings, in some faded picture book
from childhood, going headlong through the dark
to some new realm, where no mere man is king.

The sudden shift into a mythopoeic space registers, directly enough, the struggle to transcend the material constraints of working class life – the striving for another possible world. A similar metamorphosis occurs in the second verse, which focuses on Sylvia Pankhurst herself, and takes us from the detail of her day-to-day struggles to a shared epiphany, evoking Stanley Spencer's painting of the resurrection in Cookham Churchyard :

> The marches are done with,
> the hunger strikes, danger of death
>
> forgotten, as the sun cuts through the fog
> and all the world cycles away, like risen souls
>
> made new and tender for the life to come
> in some lost Resurrection Of The Body.

Cycling as a metaphor of a better life to come, but in this world, rather than the next, offers us a vision of sport as a kind of meta-physical education, the body's own way of transcendence and one that is not the prerogative of privilege.

Carol Ann Duffy's poem is also preoccupied with questions of aspiration, disadvantage and their long legacy, for, as she says in the opening line of her poem 'the past is all around us, in the air', and, she later reminds us, it 'still dedicates to us/its distant, present light'. Her approach to the East End's heritage as a source of Olympic inspiration is characteristically oblique. Anyone expecting a lyrical ode to the joys of paralympic tennis and the struggle to overcome physical disability is in for a disappointment. Instead she has written a poem about the Eton Manor Boys Club whose sports premises once occupied the site that is now to be dedicated to tennis and hockey.

To fully grasp what is at stake in her poem we have to understand something of the back story.[6] The club was founded by a group of Old Etonians in the 1880s as part of a broader civilising mission on the part of the upper classes to establish community settlements and youth clubs in the most deprived areas of the East End, where, as one of the Club's founders put it:

> boys are yearly turned loose, without aid, without sympathy, without exercise, without amusement, into the burning fiery furnace of the streets of our growing and densely-crowded cities. When they fall into sin and ruin, as so many of them do – when they pass from betting and gambling (a sin fearfully on the increase) into dishonesty and crime, or when they pass from levity and godlessness into the

abyss of yet more misery and destruction, there is no-one to offer them help or social encouragement.

The founders saw themselves as pioneers entering an 'unknown country'. One of them recorded in his diary: 'Having searched diligently through "Mogg's Guide to London and the Suburbs" for the correct geographical position of Hackney Wick, and all the Metropolitan timetables for a suitable train to Victoria Park Station, I duly started off one evening in search of adventures in the Wild East....'

But these colonists of the working class city quickly turned the area in 'their' manor. As urban slummers with a social mission their main charitable aim was to inculcate their public school ethos amongst the lower orders through various forms of rational recreation and self improvement, including sport; in particular they wanted to change the anarchic, clandestine street gang into a well-organised, highly visible and socially responsible presence in the community. To this end members of the club were organised into 'houses' to encourage team spirit and healthy competition; regular attendance and the highest standards of behaviour were also expected. The club bought a large derelict site in Hackney Wick and transformed it into the most lavishly equipped sports facility in London, which they called, without a trace of irony 'the Wilderness'. The club excelled in boxing and athletics, producing a bevy of Olympic medallists and certainly succeeded in tapping into the role that sport plays in deprived communities whose access to social mobility by other means is blocked. It offered other perks too – if you were unemployed the guvnors might find you a job.

Eton Manor closed its doors in 1967, although it still leads a vigorous afterlife in the form of an old boys' network of east Enders who remain loyal to its traditions. But that is not the end of its story. Eton Manor has a very contemporary message. Upper class philanthropy and Tory paternalism are being re-invented under the populist rubric of the 'Big Society'. So while the State is rolled back and public services, including the youth service, are savagely cut, the Hooray Henries are being urged to do good works amongst the freshly impoverished poor as 'community volunteers'.

This then is the complicated history which our Poet Laureate has chosen to explore. How has she gone about it? Largely, it has to be said, by ignoring or glossing over its more problematic aspects. The poem begins promisingly enough with an evocation of its chosen mise-en-scene. Hackney Wick is all: 'fleas, flies, bin-lids, Clarnico's Jam; the poor/enclosed by railway, marshland, factories, canal.'

We are in the City's edgelands, that inbetween space where the planners' writ no longer runs, and whose surreal ecology has been lyrically described by Paul Farley and Michael Symmons Roberts in their recent book as 'England's true wilderness'.[7] But Duffy's Wilderness, for all that it is a landscape of exclusion, is going to be reclaimed for other purposes. Thanks to the Old Etonians, it becomes a 'glorious space' connecting 'the power of place to human hope'. The response of the locals is one of amazement and gratitude in the one line in the poem where their voice is directly heard: 'Blimey, it's fit for a millionaire.'

I kept listening for a tinge of irony in the poem but it is all grace notes: 'translated poverty to self-esteem/camaraderie, and optimism similed in smiles.' Her definition of legacy is equally soft-centred: 'young lives respected, cherished, valued, helped/to sprint, swim, bowl, box, play, excel, belong/believe community is self in multitude.' It reads more like a paraphrase of the Club's mission statement or even a manifesto for the Big Society than an engagement with the complex poetics of working class aspiration described in John Burnside's poem, while the re-definition of community in such individualistic terms is bound to cause controversy in certain circles. Perhaps it is not surprising then, that the 'past all around us' has melted into air that rhymes with million.

The poem's closing lines, celebrating the continuity of this tradition of sponsored aspiration, contains its most powerful and also, for me, most problematic imagery:

> The same high sky,
> same East End moon, above this reclaimed wilderness,
> where relay boys are raced by running ghosts

The sudden appearance of a spectral geography does not disturb the elegiac sense of a wilderness reclaimed. These ghosts are not about to haunt the Games with their uncanny presence, or spoil the Olympic dream that 'everyone is a winner' with their message of lives unredeemed by private philanthropy. They have been recruited to run for Team UK and they are simply there to spur the athletes on.

Lyric poetry is made for celebration, but what is celebrated about the Olympics or East London's rich political and cultural heritage is a matter of moral as well as aesthetic judgement. All the poems, in their different ways, attempt to interpret the aspirational agenda of 2012 in terms that are consistent with the poet's own voice and vision and they will certainly make visitors to the Olympic Park reflect on what the place meant to now long-vanished communities, whose legacy of struggle is only dimly recognised in the official rhetorics of London 2012. In doing so, they honour poetry's special vocation to unsettle the official discourse, and, to varying degrees, ask awkward questions, in an idiom that can never be recuperated by beautifying lies.

Acknowledgement
Thanks to *Winning Words* for permission to quote from the commissioned poems for the Olympic Park. More information about the project can be obtained from their website , which also contains a useful anthology of poems on sporting and Olympic themes.
See www.winningwordspoetry.com

[1] This essay is based on a chapter in a forthcoming book *From the Far Side of the Tracks: studies in narrative landscape and other scenes* to be published by Routledge in 2013.

[2] For a discussion of this, see Phil Cohen 'A Beautifying Lie ? Kitsch and the 2012 Olympics' in *Soundings* 50, 2012

[3] See the contributions to Hugh Canham and Carole Satyamurti (eds) *Acquainted with the Night: psychoanalysis and the poetic imagination* (London: Karnac Books 2003).

[4] Henri de Montherlant wrote several lyrical books about the Olympics and sport. His most explicit is *Paysage des Olympiques* (Paris: Grasset 1940).

[5] Kit Wright *Hoping it might be so Poems 1974-2008* (London: Faber and Faber 2008).

[6] For further information see Michelle Johansen 'Adventures in the Wild East – The early Years of the Eton Manor Boys' Club' available online at www.villierspark.org.uk

[7] Paul Farley and Michael Symmonds Roberts *Edgelands: journeys into England's true wilderness (*London: Jonathan Cape 2011).

George Watson

Commonplaces

We know so little about how poets write. They have no interest, after all, in telling. 'The poet thinks with his poem,' said William Carlos Williams in his *Autobiography* (1951), and 'in that lies his thought.' Trespassers are not encouraged. The only extensive evidence from classical antiquity is Donatus's life of Virgil, which four centuries after the poet's death recounts how Virgil drafted his great poem in prose and on his deathbed repeatedly changed his mind about letting the *Aeneid* see the light. He died in 19 BC, leaving the decision to others, and nobody knows what changes he made or had in mind. Skip a millennium and more, and Ben Jonson remarked to William Drummond on his walking tour to Scotland in 1618-19 that his revered Westminster schoolmaster, William Camden, had taught him to write his poems first in prose. He does not say how far (if at all) he took his advice. There is a fragmentary poem by Thomas Gray called 'The Alliance of Education and Government' which appeared after his death in 1771 with a prose précis that is longer than the poem, but the instance is not inspiring.

Then the temperature rises sharply. Wordsworth spoke of emotion recollected in tranquillity, Coleridge and Robert Lowell left voluminous notes, and there are plenty of scattered remarks from recent interviews. They do not offer a convincing image, however, of what happens. The muse of poetry is inviolate.

*

There is still the commonplace book, abandoned since the seventeenth century, and it may be useful to explain what it was.

A commonplace book, based on stiff boards, waxed and erasable, was a notebook or 'table', as Shakespeare called it, (cf. *Two Gentlemen of Verona* II.7), set out with familiar headings like the seven deadly sins or the cardinal virtues. Ideally alphabetical, it is distinct from a journal or diary, which is chronological, and it could gather personal reflections as well as allusions and quotations. A humanistic form, it makes no claim to originality, being based on the assumption of the unchanging human heart, and it has no truck with multiculturalism. Montaigne's essays are plainly the product of one or several such notebooks, and Ben Jonson owned a copy of the first edition of 1580 which proudly survives, his signature inked on the title-page.

He kept one himself, what is more, which survived his death in 1637 and appeared four years later as *Timber: or Discoveries*. The order may not be his, however, and there is no way of knowing if he authorized it. Robert Southey's commonplace book was published a few years after his death as Poet Laureate in 1844, but without applause.

That makes the commonplace book look like an extinct sub-species of data-processing, and extinct long before Internet. There is more, however, to be said. In his 77th sonnet Shakespeare left so acute an account that it is hard to doubt he kept one himself.

> Look what thy memory cannot contain
> Commit to these waste blanks, and thou shalt find
> Those children nursed, delivered from thy brain,
> To take a new acquaintance of thy mind

which explains what a 'table' may have meant to him and what it was for. It could prompt creation in unexpected and unpredicted ways, in action as well as thought. Shaken by his father's ghost, Hamlet vows hysterically to wipe away 'all trivial, fond records' from the table of his memory,

> And thy commandment all alone shall live
> Within the book and volume of my brain,
> Unmixed with baser matter
>   (I.v).

The commonplace book for Hamlet is no longer an object at all, whether table or notebook, but a metaphor of mind and the will to act.

In the eighteenth century the fashion faded among writers, along with a taste for proverbs and wise instances. They sound hopelessly countrified. The conversations reported by Boswell in his life of Johnson do not use them, and poets mocked them. In *The Dunciad* (1728) Pope imagined the king of the dunces presiding over his own works, where 'a folio commonplace / Founds the whole pile, of all his works the base' (I 139-40), and ten years later, in *Polite Conversation*, Swift satirized those who supposed they could pass off familiar sayings as wit. Proverbs were banal, by then, and proverbs decorated with classical precedents merely pretentious. In *Tom Jones* (1749) Fielding has Squire Western's chaplain Mr Supple struggle to pacify him in his rage with choice classical instances, 'enriched with many valuable quotations from the ancients, particularly from Seneca' (VI 9), but it only makes things worse. The commonplace, with or without instances, had had its day, and nowadays 'What I always say ....' can start a stampede for the door.

*

The death of the commonplace in recent centuries has left a lot of literature looking opaque, however, and not only Montaigne. The first great novel in Europe, Cervantes' *Don Quixote* (1605-15), contrasts the proverbial wisdom of Sancho Panza with the follies of his learned master. Quixote is a fool because he has read too many books: a victim of the introduction of printing more than a century before, and advance warning of what can happen from radio, TV and Facebook. The growth of higher education, too, must bear some responsibility here. Montaigne and Shakespeare did not change their minds down the years but enriched them. The pace of dogmatic change began to race after the French Revolution with those who, like Wordsworth and Coleridge, were disillusioned with Napoleon. Victorian writers had religious doubts, and in the wake of those doubts ideologies like Marx and Darwin began to thrive. Writers born after 1900 are likely to have entertained far more illusions than theology or the classless society, and in 1953 Isaiah Berlin sounded a warning in *The Hedgehog and the Fox*. The metaphor is a little misleading, since hedgehogs know only one thing all their lives – how to save themselves if a predator attacks. The modern hedgehog, by contrast, believes in a succession of things, as Ronald Dworkin illustrates in *Justice for Hedgehogs,* and that is just the trouble. Many poets, in an age of advancing longevity, now look back on the follies of their youth and middle age in shame and distaste. Ezra Pound lived to call anti-semitism a vulgar suburban prejudice, and W.H. Auden maddened his publisher by insisting in his later years on revision when asked for a reprint. We know a lot about what poets eventually came to think of their poems. But what did they think as they wrote?

*

The rebirth of the commonplace is an unlikely prospect, however, and the commonplace book will remain an extinct species firmly anchored in another age.

It has lost is habitat, after all, and its food supply. T.S. Eliot achieved it occasionally, as in 'Death by water' in *The Waste Land*, which commemorates mortality: 'A current under sea / picked his bones in whispers', but it is rare and lonely triumph. Two modern cults stand firmly in the way – originality and spontaneity – and for the time being they look unshakeable. In an essay known as 'Three Good Wives' (II.35) Montaigne insists that his stories had all been true, forebade invention and recommended Ovid's *Metamorphoses* as a model to writers, since Ovid trimmed and restitched old stories rather than making them up. That is another world. Originality has now been relabelled creativity, and it would be a rash critic who tried to belittle that. It is the god of the new millennium. Ben Jonson's reputation suffered a sharp decline a century ago when editors of *Timber* demonstrated it was not an original work, as Swinburne had enthusiastically supposed, but largely a mass of quotations and allusions from ancient authors and modern humanists. It is an example to give pause.

As for spontaneity, it is hard to discredit because poets often believe in it themselves. That is deeply puzzling, since they seldom practise it. But all aspire, probably because the great poems that are familiar in anthologies look totally achieved, as if by a single act. 'The master poets must come down at their poems as a hawk on a pigeon at one dive,' Archibald MacLeish once remarked, adding sadly that he could not do it himself. 'I chip away like a stone-mason.' No wonder poets sound so sad. They should try thinking of Shakespeare, or rather *Hamlet*. Or even Virgil.

Six Chosen young Broadsheet Poets

William Searle, 25, was born in Dorset. He is currently living in North Wales, Snowdonia. He was awarded an AHRC Studentship to study for a PhD in Creative Writing with Sir Andrew Motion. He is also training to be a mountaineering instructor.

The Mute Swan

He was like the first paper-aeroplane I made
then left out in the night: hefty with damp,
scrunched and chilled by strangling fists of dew,
rolling and slapping upon my heaven's beach

with every flow and undertow of morning tide.
Water burst out like kettle-steam through a hole
in his chest as if from a stranded whale's
blow-hole. Who could shoot a mute swan?

Was it some suspicious fisherman blaming
him for the year of no fish? Or did lightning
sear out the numinous flashing of his heart?
His time on earth was up, up, and down.

I dragged him by the turgid hose of his neck
through shells and sand. His wings, shrivelled
by salt, snapped back when I unfolded them
to the broad expanse they once were. Wind

rustled the once cashmere-down of his feathers
now constricted by cuffs of crust. And the smell:
egret breath, faecal, sulphuric. Guava-like blood
dribbled from the winter-wheat grain of his bill.

The ingot seed and flair of his eyes were now
pinches of mustard white. It was a staggering
commotion when he laboured to fly in an attack
of every wing-beat. Turnstones, busy in the kelp-

mats, scattered in an alarm of ear-piercing bray.
Torso of a marshland angel, caved-in and stunned
by vice of wave and star, forgive me that all I
could do was bury you in what I know: root-foyers

worming beneath a twisted oak. I firmly believe I too
will be bored through, hollowed out and hauled
into your nest of sky and twigs where you'll be clamouring
with the sun in your bill to put it where my heart is.

The April Cormorant

By the edge of a reed-bed I found her
lolling and seething for breath.

Yesterday's wind wasn't strong enough
to revive the dying blue flame of her eyes,

her wings ribboned in an opium of disease
unable to flower into flight,

unable to hug her sides in a streamline dive
for a spinning shoal-flash of fish.

Still enticed by the grey waters lapping a rock
from where she could draw her inner maps

of holy sonar across the bay, she shuffled,
gasped, gurgled to swing her head upward

toward the iron-sky's swelling bruise of rain
then collapsed, buckling under the drowsy weight

of her honey-comb bones and the leaden pressure
of my remote human eye.

I lost my faith in spring then approached on my knees
with nothing to give, no cure,

no draught of pristine oxygen to fuel her lungs,
to regenerate the swill of her cormorant blood –

she was terrified of me like a child is
of shadows growing across the wall of his room –

only a woollen cloud of blanket to fold
cold darkness around her, to softly dry her wings

while she sank deeper and deeper
into a midnight-cot of her own – holding my breath

as I carried her unbearably light body – breathing again
when I passed her over into a stranger's hands.

The Stone Wall

Gwilym Jones, daily you decline my helping hand
to restore the old stone wall around your farm.

A crow is pecking out an injured ewe's eyes,
tearing her teats that spill milk into the mud.
Her lamb is crying out from Clogwyn Mawr.
The cuckoo's flute is out of tune.

You bare your toothless grin
while sparring with an open fire, peeling back mole-skins
with your thumb-nail as though they were
black, deformed potatoes.

An adder's skin floats by on the wind.
Swallows, nattering and defecating upon your gable-end,
will die in their nests you stuff full with poison.

Snowdon is a god keeping a watchful eye
upon your dour, pebble-dash house – an igloo of rust –
swallowed by waves of diesel, bracken and sprockets.

Dog chains rattle in the rainfall of night.
Big Bear crouches over your sleeping mare.

Look, Gwilym, your son is moping back from school,
tired from bullying foreign kids,
scuffing his feet though a desert of gravel,
munching broken biscuits of slate, gargling soot.

At night, you wake to the screams of his night-terrors.
In a gown of bandages and barbed-wire, you limp
outside and fire your shotgun at dark, winged figures
breathing heavily in the trees.

Sarah Holland-Batt was born in Surfers Paradise, Queensland in 1982 and has lived in Australia, the United States, Italy and Japan. Her first book of poems, *Aria* (University of Queensland Press), won the Judith Wright Poetry Prize, the Thomas Shapcott Prize and the FAW Anne Elder Award, and was shortlisted in both the Queensland and New South Wales Premiers' Literary Awards. She is the recipient of an Australia Council Literature Residency at the B.R. Whiting Studio, the Marten Bequest Travelling Scholarship, the Dorothy Hewett Fellowship, and an Asialink Literature Residency. In late 2010 she was the W.G. Walker Memorial Fulbright Scholar at New York University.

Rosser Park

This is no place. Our bamboo thicket's
been razed for rosebuds
and the honeymooners with picnic plates and cups
have waned and shrivelled up.
The wooded jetty where I drove you for walks
is sloppy now, rotting on its stilts,
and I am in disrepair, wintered out.
The old pond has greened,
a stinking algae steeps the water weeds.
Globes of purple garlic flower fall to seed.
Old griefs flare and fire in the mind.
I remember waterspiders on the lilies,
stale standoffs, your tartan flask of tea.
The harlequin ducks who painted circles
on the water's sullen surface are fled.
Father, how can I say what I cannot see,
the failure of fountains and botany,
lotus buds drowned in mangrove muck,
the pointlessness of a pair of swans
preening on an artificial island's rocks.

The House on Stilts

Through weaved air, that wedge of darkness
chocked beneath our weatherboard

was no man's land – a fretwork of lattice
checkerboarded the sun, and a fernery

of maidenhairs and birdsnests drifted
round the edges, tinting the light green.

An underground exile, I cupped my ear
upwards for the thud of clipped heels

knocking like ghosts through the floorboards.
Now I am the ghost, back down where

the heron-house, the crane-house dips
its white sticks into mud, where the black rats

scuffle at night in old fuel cans, where lengths
of fishing line fray on copper nails

and film-eyed possums drag their claws.
Born between the wars, between the grey fringe

of scrub and the glass scrawl of reef, this
white ghost-crab tiptoed a century, metal-backed,

and now is history. The gulf yawns – a lifetime
since cyclone rain rattled the venetians

like a handful of thumbtacks, discord
of a continent, but I am there still,

midden-deep, and the light flickers
in and out around me like radio static.

A salt breeze has withered the passionflower;
it hangs dead on the vine. The moon flattens to a crisp.

Hang, we will all hang. Night comes early here;
midges jag in the sky like anxious stars.

Poem for my Father at Sanssouci

The vineyards tumble downhill, nobody knows where.
Rain comes and goes, it is impossible to rely on.
Our quiet garden paths of snapdragon and hedge
lead to the weeping tree; its branches sweep the ground.
An eagle's stone eye stares over the water
and the slow herd of clouds turns north to Berlin.
Life is not yet over. The red rococo silk
still curls with fleur de lis, putti cling
to the ceiling and don't remember why.
A terrible purity moves in the high leaves.
It's worse that way, to live for centuries.
Better to wipe the long rooms of childhood clean,
grey hours in Harrogate, buried bottles of whisky.
One by one they fly out like sweet wrappers
into the blue sky, the grey sky, small suicides.
No one will lead you, no one will follow you
when you migrate to darker eaves.
I have seen the swallows foraging there
for winter material in the meagre fibres.
They gather twigs and drop their feathers.
That is their sadness, they ask for nothing.
Death will find them in the high towers
where they wait in makeshift nests;
the wind will seal their eyes together
so they forget even the light, and shut it out.

Dom Knox-Crawford, 22, is a student at the University of Sussex, studying for an MA in Modern and Contemporary Literature. He is currently working on a translation of Karel Čapek's *The English Letters*, as well as his first collection of poems *Jupiter*, which is on the history of the National Grid from 1950 onwards. His inspiration stems from the changes of natural landscape, to modern political events and anthropology.

Dungeness

I watch the water throwing out its arms
of wave-beaten driftwood; miles scarp
into a carpet of teeth, the teeth into sea,
the sea into a sliver we call 'horizon'.

– Heave, suck, then another heave –
as it gobbles the beach with greed.
Then he left, with a succulent smack
kissing rocks, rolling back again.

Salvaging earth with a spade against
the swell; as they labour, feet in pools
of spume, malarial and sweet-smelling,
carving out this small, grey Eden;

raising with their brutal, strong hands,
the virgin land (the moody suitor-sea
showering a dowry of glints from afar).
As a fossil clinging to rock, Dungeness.

Alone. A miasma of silence, concrete,
criss-crossed spider webs; slumber.
We cut a ditch to vein away the sea,
like sleep rounding onto a tired brain; then

we must call it a night. It is the panther
and Neptune coming to eat our world.

Vileweed

'And if you mingle among the acorns the seeds of Genista spinosa, or furs, they
will come up without any damage, and for a while needs no other fence, and will be
kill'd by the shade of the young oaklings before they become able to do them any
prejudice.'

John Evelyn: Sylva

Before dimpling out the earth, to the scattering of compost
in spongy handfuls, to the ways of ordering, ablaqueation,
the husbandman will carefully choose his patch. Then, a

seminar of sylvans (the accordance of the four elements
being met; neither *too keen or sharp, too cold or hot;
not infected with foggs and poys'nous vapours*) bulk out

like strong hand-muscles from the ground, fingers opening
in gestures, half spoken silent languages. 'Husband',
they say; 'bring us a sacrifice, a locket of golden broom.'

The gardener plants this cruelty around his saps, bracelets
of a weaker sex, or genus. And while the field mouse tears
at their Promethean patience, the saplings grow, quietly

from imps to imperial, sapping all elements from the broom-
moat (the gardener happily quotes Cato, Theophrastus,
buys pamphlets dealing with *The Nature of the Cacktus*) –

whilst Vileweed dies, gnawed to death and starved of light.
While the bastard brood of oaks outgrow the nursery, and man,
like a silent witness, gleams at the treasure of their crown.

Garlic

First, he weighed the half pound
of silver moons, turning them over in his rich fingers,

then chucked the lot in a bucket, a dull thunder.
And their skins cracked into confetti, and some split,

magnificent white-purple hearts rolling on the tarmac.
And the villagers' wives, heads wrapped in red scarves

talking of births and marriages turned into myths,
and a hand, dipping and adding and taking away,

those cloves in their simple globes
opening like blessings.

Seán Hewitt, 21, is reading English at Girton College, Cambridge, where he was awarded the Rima Alamuddin Prize for Poetry in 2011. He is the current Editor-in-Chief, and co-founder of *The Tower*, a poetry magazine based in Cambridge. Alongside this, his poetry has been anthologised in *The Mays XIX*, and published in *Northwords Now, Crannóg, The Journal, Erbacce,* and elsewhere. You can find out more by visiting his blog at seanhewitt.blogspot.com

Speech Therapy

The ground, stubborn as a turnip,
Sat under our shoes. With all the
Kissing-gate awkwardness of sheep,

We looked upwards at the wild
Progeny of earth. Whoever
Named the birds had a mouth made

For England: Nuthatch, Woodlark,
Willow-warbler, we'd seen them all
And heard god chime bells in their throats.

Like kites, we held them with our eyes
On thread, long and diaphanous.
We guided their flight from the ground

In silence, ballasted by thoughts
That lay in our stomachs like stones.
Then the wind changed. Our eye-strings,

Crossed by the oilvoiced birds, tangled
And threaded into sailors' knots,
So we almost swallowed our tongues.

Holding still, speaking through teeth and lip,
I told you what to do: Let go of words,
Cut the string. We did, and we could sing.

From *Presents from Papua*

                i

Have you ever seen the light
When a man's eyes turn to marbles?
The day he got his M.B.E.
They were ponds in which shadows swam.

Light-talk left the darkness celibate:
There was no forest-herb fit
To fix us for the Queen's gaze –
We knew to whom our taxes went.

In the car, someone joked
Whilst Ireland and Papua sat
Bondaged and gagged in the boot.
Protest shirt was swapped for suit,

They listened to old IRA songs
And thought about that fourth green field,
But flicked back to BBC as London
Approached in all its moneyed glory.

He was middle-named on radio,
Even smiled for Charles as the medal
Pinched his chest, then turned home,
Head still bowed like a heavy-seeded flower.

ii

'Don't look at me,' he said to the Sun.
'The royal swan flew me home
From Papua, and its darkness
Bruised the haunted spine of snow

That lay between the runway lights.
Now, in the sweat of morning,
You tease me back from the miles
I went in my dreams. See my mouth,

Wide like a split pomegranate,
Dry from last night's drink, the wound
Of Europe in my sleepmapped skin.
Here money spits flintcurses at

The feet of homelessness, and life
Itself addles my brain. I am soused
With the quench of alcohol, and
Not even you can wrench me

From my bed. The heat-hazed quietudes
Of afternoons and the horse's flyshake
Won't betray your hot perniciousness.
Come, peel me apart like a poached rabbit.'

Ian Harker is twenty eight and was born and lives in Leeds. He is a bookseller, a founder of LIPP*fest*, currently chairs the Leeds Writers Circle, and edits poetry for the *Cadaverine*.

Earthwork

They laboured by hand –
month after month of hacking up the earth
and piling it steep to make a top
where the wind smacks you in the face.
They went as deep as they went high,
cutting off the headland from sea to sea,
nothing but sea at their backs and in front
of them the dyke.

                And it's still there,
older than we ever thought. You can look
down, like they did, and watch people
coming up. And behind it the rich soil
and all that flint, pegged out
by hedges and roads. The earth struggles
and we fight it back.

Tree

Listen. Can you hear the hiss in the wiring?
There's Arabic in the leaves and the wind talking
in the twigs. Can you feel the lilt in your ears
as you get close? That's the pressure singing its way
to the sky, saying every loop in this cylinder
is a sunrise. You won't drag it over.

It holds a hand out in the dark to go up,
bark scabbing into skin. The leaves find sight
and the sap follows, there's a thud in the taproot
balancing into a heartbeat, a heart's chambers
wide and then shut in the heartwood. Hold still.
Those branches are bending into arms.

Nets

They told her to stop feeding the birds.
But their wings were eyelids
as earth retreated
and the snow filled it.

Any noise, however slight, could bring them,
waving over the hedge
and wanting the ground-rent.

The phone rang
but the cord was out.
The gas went off
but it was still so hot.

Taps spat and juddered
and she was sure it was them –
no ghost could take your house like this.

They were in the walls now
and there were shadows in the hall.
Soon there would be only one room,
the windows out
and the doors nailed shut.

Kaddy Benyon, 38, was born and raised in East Anglia. She worked as a television scriptwriter prior to having children. She was recently awarded a distinction for her Creative Writing MA and is hoping to start a PhD later this year. Her poetry has appeared in *Ambit, Mslexia, the London Magazine, Popshot, the Frogmore Papers,* and *Stand.* She was shortlisted for the Fish Poetry Prize 2010, the Picador Poetry Prize 2011, the Cinnamon Poetry Award 2011 & 2012 and the Crashaw Prize 2012. Twitter - @KaddyBenyon

Palm House

Your grandmother says you teetered
all day – spiked shrieks provoking
glasshouse sweat – *a feverish
temperament,* she said. I sensed
a cyclone under the lip of your wilting
hat and plucked you from a canopy of jade

vine and steamed panes to a bright, wide
lawn where you pirouetted a fountain,
limp daisies chained at your neck.
I clapped and you bowed,
frowned then see-sawed a wet ledge,
cocking your head as you finger-dipped

to dissolve a murky twin. Now, sweetheart,
there is only this: the clack, clack
of your saccharine clock,
you rocking hot, sticking to my breast,
my tips untangling each knot
of your spine. I nuzzle your damp neck,

its fuzzy scent of roots, algae and sun,
yet your moist chest judders still,
pulsing doubts into me. I trace your clammy
heart line and wish I could offer you more
than this parched and arid time
with its heat; the sweltering heat.

Milk Fever

You, my Inuit mother – those
low-slung cheeks, watery eyes hidden
inside a fur-lined hood, breasts you
couldn't unpack in time for your milk

to be supped unfrozen. You strapped
me to a sled, wrapped tight in pelts,
a matted fleece, some buckskin
stretched and dried that summer

you grew me inside you. A reek
of hunt and meat, a thick blood
pulsing the air with each numb thud
of your snow boots kicking up ice,

glittering my hair. North you trekked,
the sled ropes tied to your waist
as you grunted, sweat and chapped.
All I wanted was for you to stop,

hold me still a moment, not leave
me tethered to a lumber pole
as you hacked pale blue blocks, stacked
them to build a snow-dome shelter.

You lit a fire in its pit, heated meltwater
in a wide, silver bowl and held it
steaming wildly to my lips. Head dipped,
you left me in a darkness of sniffing

bear and fox, like a dream, a fear
I wake from: drifts of white linen, you
asleep nose-to-nose with me, almost
invisible, mere breath on my face.

Undone

We had to run for the bus after confession,
where waiting for Mother's silence
I'd made imaginary idols of saints, illuminated

by twenty votives I paid for with flickers
of prayer. We'd no time for my litany
of lies and spite and rage so the priest winked

and told me *Next time*. I reached for Mother's
hand, already crammed with beads
clacking together: a metronome for OCD.

Her illness worshipped muttering; stations
of the cross mostly but then anything
with a repeating pattern, lost in a hail of Marys.

She let me sit by the window, while, head
bowed she vowed to settle breaths above
the throb and grind of engine. Her hands knitted

together then apart, twisting and fidgeting inside
deliberate sleeves. She looked as odd
as the panting man in the soiled mac, uncurtaining

bushes when we stopped at lights. He grinned
up at me, presenting his puffy, purpley
grub. I covered up my eyes and whispered:

How soon is next time Mummy? Mum?

Zoe Brigley

Reviewing Neglected Younger Poets
Part 1: Mythmakers and Breakers

Leanne O'Sullivan: *Cailleach, the Hag of Beara* (Bloodaxe, 2009)
Paul Kingsnorth: *Kidland and Other Poems* (Salmon, 2011).
Emily Berry: *Stingray Fevers* (Tall Lighthouse, 2008)
Sinéad Wilson: *The Glutton's Daughter* (Donut Press, 2006)
Sasha Dugdale: *Red House* (Carcanet, 2011)
Meirion Jordan: *Moonrise* (Seren, 2008)

In the past few years, youth has been a significant word for British poetry canon-makers. James Byrne's and Claire Pollard's *Voice Recognition* focused mainly on younger writers, while this year Salt brought out *The Salt Book of Younger Poets* co-edited by Roddy Lumsden and Eloise Stonborough. Finally, Todd Swift and Kim Lockwood are bringing out an anthology in 2012 of young poets for Oxfam titled *Lung Jazz*. The remit of this essay is to take a closer look at some alternative younger poets who may have fallen in the cracks between anthologies, or who may not have received as much attention as they deserve. I do so on the proviso that it is not only the 'young' who are 'breaking into' poetry or producing ground-breaking work. The review, however, is written in the spirit of giving new work by younger poets more attention than a one-hundred-word mention in a standard round-up.

All the poets have been highlighted by *Agenda* in the online Broadsheets, as well as in the journal itself, and all of them have distinct and arresting voices which merit further scrutiny. In order to represent them as fully as possible, I have split the poets into three categories: 'Mythmakers and Breakers,' 'Social Anatomists' and 'Cartographers'. These categories are not meant to reduce the writers' unique personalities. Nor are they an attempt at creating a canon. They are simply a way of organizing a group of diverse voices, and it is perhaps the differences between the writers in each category that are most intriguing.

Leanne O'Sullivan's debut collection *Waiting for my Clothes* provided moving portraits of personal vulnerability, but her most recent, *Cailleach, the Hag of Beara*, uses the same probing emotional scrutiny in a mythical context. The Cailleach Bhéarra is a mythical hag in Irish (and Scottish) legend who stands for the nation, but O'Sullivan's version becomes an authentic, flawed human woman. Challenging nationalist icons of women in Irish discourse, O'Sullivan gives the Cailleach context and humanity, setting out five stages of her life through birth, sex, sibling rivalry, desire, and old age. The poems also explore how and why myths are created. As O'Sullivan comments in an untitled prose poem: 'Age continues with its backwards glances, with all its ghosts and one layer of stone settles on another.' The layers of rock refer to the legend of the Cailleach's birth from stone, but the image also gestures to the caprices of history where 'backwards glances' become permanent, immovable strata. O'Sullivan considers how gossip and innuendo solidify into mythologies or histories. So in 'Rumour,' when the neighbours gossip, the Cailleach explains: 'The rumours didn't end, became gestures, / like branches nodding.' The rumours imagined as the wind in the trees suggest that gossip-mongering is as fundamental as breath. O'Sullivan's storytelling, however, focuses on the Cailleach's humanity, especially when she finds a lover, who is not a god as in the old tales, but a fisherman. The poems that describe their relationship celebrate the palpable joy of physical and emotional love. In 'The Unwhispered Hush,' the Cailleach describes her lover as 'the first thought the world had / when it dipped its palms and made rivers' making 'everything suddenly, beautifully, touchable.' The splendour of this description makes it very poignant when the Cailleach's lover dies. In 'Her Husband Says,' her lost love comforts her from beyond the grave:

> I said that the leaves will come,
> deep green shadows
>
> rising over the frost after I am gone.
> I told you that you would stand here again

Through representing the Cailleach's delights and tragedies, O'Sullivan conjures a human woman who is defiant, passionate, and indomitable. She also defies the archetype of the crone or Mother Ireland, and ultimately, the Cailleach is far more complex than traditional myths have admitted.

O'Sullivan's collection is in a long tradition of Irish women rewriting myths to humanize women, but Paul Kingsnorth's collection, *Kidland*, uses myth in a decidedly more masculine way. Reminiscent of Ted Hughes, Kingsnorth focuses on the primitive side of nature and human life. *Kidland* also references Robinson Jeffers and Rainer Maria Rilke as influences. Like Jeffers, Kingsnorth describes the futility of human life on the world stage, and, similar to Rilke, he admires nature's lack of self-consciousness, a very human quality. The most successful poems represent the chilling dynamic between predator and prey in natural and human worlds. There is a primal sensibility to the poetry when Kingsnorth speaks in the voice of 'The bird killer' whose prey 'is warm and moves in my hands / like a newborn. I do not have to. I have to.' The bird's destruction is as horrifying as infanticide, yet Kingsnorth suggests that the death is inevitable. The urge to be merciful is always overridden by the desire to kill. Kingsnorth reiterates this message again in the poem 'stalker' but from the point of view of the prey. The quarry is described in unpunctuated, breathless lines: 'flat in the hollow press your ears to your back still your wings pray / that he passes.' Kingsnorth concludes about the hunter: 'You will kill because you must.' This drive to kill is also applied to human worlds – to English history in 'Angles' and to Nazi philosophy in 'Master Race', but most of all it is mapped out in the long title poem. 'Kidland' is a kind of modern myth which recalls Freud's theories of the death drive and his view of the child or primitive as a mass of violence and desire. In 'Kidland', drives for death and pleasure run wild, working as an antidote to sterile metropolitan life, because modern subjects are

[...] a leaden race, a numb people
nursing our yellow volumes while America's empire
smothers us with its dying breath.

Most disturbing is the encounter between Sarah, a tourist, and an anonymous 'Green Man' who represents the chaotic wilderness of Kidland. What begins as a conversation between Sarah and the man ends in a rape, and there is something distasteful about Kingsnorth using sexual violence in this way. Kingsnorth does try to shift the power binaries, describing the man as 'Small and violated,' while Sarah thinks 'You are in my power now.' The following passage, however, is rather disturbing:

You did it because you wanted to, because you could,
because you are an animal, because you will escape. You did it
because this is what men do when the walls are lowered and the ropes
removed. Applaud yourself; you have shown an honesty tonight
that few men show.

Is Kingsnorth questioning why men rape? What are his conclusions? What is this modern myth trying to tell us? Does it offer new insights or is it merely the same old message that men are at the mercy of their 'drives'? Many questions are left unanswered and such mythologizing works on dangerous ground.

Another poet writing through mythology, violence and violation is Emily Berry in *Stingray Fevers*. If Kingsnorth recalls Hughes' primitive tricksters, Berry's voices are certainly reminiscent of Plath's poems like 'Lady Lazarus' where masochism and defiance meet. Berry, however, does not just produce pastiches of Plath, but develops her own specific approach. Most often, her narrators give themselves away – their anxieties, their failings – without realizing it. By using this technique, Berry engages ironically with gender issues, myths about sexuality and bourgeois attitudes. For example, when the narrator describes her hero in 'Vignette', stating 'He was like a *total prophet*,' the modish language creates bathos which undermines the voice's authority. Other poems are more sinister in their implications. The narrator of 'A Short Guide to Corseting' describes her compliance to her lover's desire: 'We agreed small waists were more attractive; / we were in a loving and supportive relationship.' In this and other poems, the narrators' insistence on their own masochistic choices is portrayed in a menacing manner. Often these women are giving up control of their own bodies, as in the Bluebeard story 'A Piece of You', where a lover chides his masochistic beloved 'Why did you provoke me, when I always wanted to be gentle?' Violence and coercion are also redolent in 'Things Fall Apart' where the foreboding and despair of Yeats and Achebe are transferred to a mundane, domestic setting and a destructive relationship. Berry explains: 'He didn't hurt her physically. She hurt herself, / fist to the wall, a bruise like a spillage.' Like Kingsnorth, Berry creates a kind of Freudian mythology which intimates the frightening power dynamic between the violater and violated, the hunter and prey. Berry's irony, however, reveals how coercion works without glamourizing it.

Spanning the gap between Kingsnorth and Berry is the myth-making of Sasha Dugdale in her most recent collection *Red House*. Dugdale is a librettist who creates decorous and stylish poetry, and in this collection in particular she draws on Anna Akhmatova and Marina Tsvetaeva. To create the dark, vital world of the 'red house,' Dugdale draws on the startling imagination of these Russian poets. She also maintains a vivid sense of history, moving between time periods to interrogate legends – real or mythical – of violence, cruelty and civilization. The title poem explains that the house is 'made of wasp-thought and saliva.' If the red house was a church it has long since been abandoned, but Dugdale ironically employs sacred imagery to describe a godless community. 'On Beauty' for example, is a litany that pleads for a haven from violation, poverty and imperialism:

> Lord, give me the strength to protect these children
> From the soliders, ex-soldiers, arse fuckers, shitmongers
> The unclean, unwashed, the simple, the hopeless, the West
> With its bulbous self-determination.

The speaker laments with parental concern, but some of the threats listed are ambiguous. When the voice denounces 'arse fuckers', is this the voice of bigot deriding alternative sexualities? How trustworthy is the storyteller who presents this myth? It is difficult to ascertain the speaker's reliability, but, like Paul Kingsnorth, Dugdale emphasises the lack of certainty in Western ideologies. There is anxiety too that the current status quo might be overturned to be replaced by something worse. In 'Maldon', Dugdale references the Battle of Maldon in Essex, England when the Vikings defeated the Anglo-Saxons. The narrator describes how 'a new race / Has come up out of the sea, dripping with gold, crueller than the last.' Dugdale's poems reel with horror at the violence of the world and express this horror in mythical terms. In 'Asylum', Penelope describes the state of things after Odysseus's return home, and the carnage after his homecoming merely continues the cycle of destruction and violence:

> The prostitutes hang from a beam like mice.
> The suitors are piled unburied in the yard.
> And some say that it is now much better
> And others, that it is worse.

The world of the mythical red house is one of discord, hence Dugdale's 'A Ballad without Rhyme'. The subject of this dissonant ballad, however, is a courageous woman, who remains standing 'wrathful, impossible to behold.' Drawing on history and myth, Dugdale creates an imperfect domain for her poems where violence is neverending, though women and poets might stand against it.

Dugdale's mythical women represent a principle beyond barbarity and violence, but Sinéad Wilson's neat chapbook *The Glutton's Daughter* is more likely to deflate myth than to create one. Drawing on classical literature, art and film, *The Glutton's Daughter* is not afraid to mix classical allusion with everyday culture. Take for example the bathos of 'Memories of Bewick Street and Dyfrig' in which London prostitutes are described via allusions to Shakespeare's *The Merchant of Venice*. Referencing Shakespeare's lead casket and its message not to judge by appearances, the narrator tells how a friend gives the local prostitute a name – not Portia, the lady won by Bassanio in the casket game, but Porsche immediately deflating the moral and classical associations. Wilson invokes Shakespeare again in 'The Tycoon's Wife', especially Romeo's comparison of Juliet to a 'rich jewel in an Ethiop's ear.' Wilson juxtaposes the wife's 'quiet black maids' and her 'jet teardrop studs,' signalling that the human maids have become just another commodity – another aspect of 'all this stolid, cold wealth.' The prostitute in 'Memories of Bewick Street and Dyfrig' and the maids in 'The Tycoon's Wife' are both rendered to mere objects. Wilson's interrogation of myth and gender is not always convincing, however. The *femme fatale* in 'Le Film Noir,' seems to merely rehash old stereotypes: 'I know these dames are dolls, / fickle as smoke that seeps from lips.' Generally though, Wilson's interrogation of myth, art and gender is exciting, complex and convincing. The title poem 'The Glutton's Daughter' is a good example. La Goulue (The Glutton) was a can-can dancer in 1890s Paris, but she also became a model for Toulouse-Lautrec's famous Moulin Rouge posters. Wilson considers the myths surrounding this real woman using a monologue from the point of view of her daughter, a step which extends the strategies of O'Sullivan, because it considers the inheritances of myth-making surrounding women. Describing how she too becomes an artist's model for Degas, the daughter affirms 'I'm no black cat trapped, / crying her fate behind his wall of paint.' Alluding to Toulouse-Lautrec's poster for Le Chat Noir, the daughter places the artist's model as muse firmly in the past, and rejects the mythical status for a more active creative role.

Wilson's deflation of myths – related to gender and art – have something in common with the wry bathos of Meirion Jordan in *Moonrise*. Wilson punctures her pumped-up mythical subjects, and Jordan's aim too is to undermine elevated and sentimental subjects. In Jordan's 'Wolf,' the narrator tells a kind of fairy tale, 'Once I was told that long ago / there were no poems, only wolves,' but concludes that 'now most bring back dog skin, badly dyed.' 'Wolf' undermines the elevated status of modern poetry, recalling the anxiety of influence. Modern poems can only be fake wolves. Such deflation can be seen in the title poem, the villanelle 'Moonrise', and its refrain, 'The moon will rise, the blue screen will console.' The mingling of the modern and the everyday with classical, poetic imagery characterizes *Moonrise* as a whole. The book also offers a mixture of poetic forms juxtaposing freer narrative forms with traditional types like the villanelle, and it mixes classical allusions to sources like Homer, Catullus and the Bible with references to popular genres like science fiction. It is difficult to know how to read poems like 'Another poem about living on Mars' where the casual title contrasts with the seemingly genuine feeling in the wish for 'rain in purple clouds rotting / through the red crust on olives.' Poems of other worlds are brought back to earth by verses on the banality and mundaneness of everyday life, such as 'Blockbuster season' and 'Pirate music'. It should not be forgotten either that Jordan is a Welsh poet; he brings his keen sense of irony to bear on the Welsh affinity with Latin America in 'The new world.' This parody conjures unlikely characters like 'Olwen Perón' to undercut nationalist myths of Wales's importance. This does not mean, however, that Jordan is a self-hating Welshman. In 'A camera at Senghenydd Pit', Jordan invokes the Senghenydd Mining Disaster:

> But there were scenes I did not capture, men
> grottoed like statues underground, the smoke's
> slow wringing of their lungs or that one searing
> flash.

The opening lines quoted above begin with an absence – the scenes that were not captured, that could never have been captured by the living. Jordan does not create a jingoistic myth of the pit disaster, but instead tries to invoke the tangible, painful experience. This strategy respects the reality of the event, without making it into fodder for nationalist myth-making.

Myth-making or myth-breaking are significant activities for all of the poets discussed here. Each one engages with cultural or traditional mythologies in order to enhance or subvert them. Leanne O'Sullivan reinvents the myth of the Cailleach Bhéarra, who becomes not just a feminine figuring of the Irish nation, but a real human woman. Paul Kingsnorth invents 'Kidland,' a mythical place that represents the primitive nature of human beings. Emily Berry taps into Freudian sexual mythologies to challenge scripts of sexual domination, while Sasha Dugdale creates in her 'Red House' a frightening myth about human nature – its inconstancies, its barbarity, as well as its beauty. Sinéad Wilson deflates gender myths about women's appetites – sexual, artistic or otherwise, while Meirion Jordan is keen to debunk grand narratives of nationalism and punctures the elevated status of poetry. All of the poets engage with the act of mythologizing or demythologizing in unique ways, and they all suggest compellingly that mythologies – for better or worse – are fundamental to how human beings perceive the world.

Editor's note: at the time of going to press, Zoe Brigley's new collection, *Conquest* (Bloodaxe, 2012) and Meirion Jordan's new collection, *Regeneration* (Seren, 2012), have just been received. These will be reviewed in the next issue of *Agenda*.

NOTES FOR BROADSHEET POETS

Peter Dale

The Light is Dark Enough

In the 1950s, aged fourteen, I knew I was going to be a poet. At that age, you may well know your destination but you've no idea of the best route and you lack handy directions to the nearest way forward. This was truer for me than perhaps for others in a similar fix since I was being brought up in a virtually bookless household with the nearest thing to poetry a hymn-book or two – but where the King James Version of the Bible was read aloud. This grounding in its rhythms was perhaps where the journey began. School was the obscure wood where I hoped the seldom trod track might show a trace or two.

The English master was an enthusiast for poetry, particularly formal verse and the works of Browning, a strange formalist. His heart was clearly in the right place but his head was elsewhere by several decades. He actually referred to Masefield as modern and the only Eliot he taught was 'La Figlia che piange'. Anyway, in one lesson, he introduced a poem by A. S. J. Tessimond, 'La Marche des machines'. He was, it seemed, expecting that, after his lessons so far, we'd be underwhelmed by this apparently modern poem. Well, not me. After Palgrave's *Golden Treasury* and Masefield, I found the poem an invigorating breath of oxygen. This poem was my curious gateway to modernism. (Tessimond did write the uncollected 'Sunweb' which takes off from Eliot's poem.)

The next shock to the system was my coming across Pound's piece, 'Villanelle: The Psychological Hour', which was baffling and left doubts whether I had what it would take to be a poet. Abandon all hope. But, as Keats said, in poetry every man must work out his own salvation and, by that time, I was spending paper-round money on the odd slim volume but, more important, on the *London Magazine*. There, if ancient memory serves me right, I encountered another poem by A. S. J. Tessimond, 'Middle-aged conversation'. (He preferred the French way of presenting titles.) Again this poem held me: it had more than enough formal honing to impress even the English master and it had the succinctness almost of a Pope couplet.

> 'Are you sad to think how often
>   You have let all wisdom go
> For a crimson mouth and rounded
>   Thighs and eyes you drown in?' 'No.'

> 'Do you find this level country,
>   Where the winds more gently blow,
> Better than the summit raptures
>   And the deep-sea sorrows?' 'No.'

– The English master should have appreciated those weighted caesuras but he was a Browning optimist.

Unsurprisingly, Tessimond's early work shows odd traces of the influences on his period: imagism, Pound, the Audenesque occasional omission of articles but I did not pick that sort of thing up then. Later, I found hints from Baudelaire, Villon and Laforgue. He was a poet of city life as his selection, *Voices in a giant city* indicates; the opening part satires on various city and other types and the later poems more inward dramatic monologues.

Frost's poem 'The Road not Taken' is, in one respect, back to front. You only know the road taken and the dozens of missed and rejected routes when you turn round, grey and and retrospective. And, from here, I can see that Tessimond's little dialogue was the splinter under the skin which I extracted as the idea of duologue that underlies several approaches that developed in my own verse. Dialogue and conversation pieces are a dominant strand in Tessimond's work, too, I learnt, where he becomes a brilliant classical generalist, somewhat isolated in the pervading 'concretist' poetics. He has been an unacknowledged early influence behind the Movementeers and even Larkin, in some respects. See his poem 'Houses' for a pointer or two but there are several other traces.

Another curious coincidence of these wanderings on and off the straight route lay in the fact that the first monolingual French book of poetry I acquired was a big volume of Jacques Prévert, a poet, as I later discovered, Tessimond has translated. – Translation, a thing I'd made a pact with myself never to do – and look where that example led?

Ironically, I later discovered how sniffily Pound had replied to Tessimond, the poet who had led me to Pound and modernism – by indirection finding direction out, the way of all poets. – But Pound had written a pretty shattering put-down for a young poet: 'Cant see that yr. work has any marked individuality, or as yet any character to distinguish it from anyone elses.' [Pound's punctuation, the letter was quoted by Hubert Nicholson in *The Collected Poems of A. S. J. Tessimond*, Autolycus, 1985.] This letter must have been received around 1928. A. S. J. was about twenty-six. Tessimond's encrypted rejoinder was perhaps 'Tube station', worth comparing with the approach in Pound's haiku-type 'On a Station of the Metro'.

In my teaching days, long-ago, Tessimond's work became invaluable in introducing teenagers to poetry. His 'Cats II' is justifiably anthologized with its unforgettable opening and closing, 'Cats no less liquid than their shadows /Offer no angles to the wind.'

The cat is, in one way and another, an image of life envied by Tessimond. – See the poem 'Night-life'. The cat shows a way through life that is without friction or commitment, but it was a way his turbulent inner self could never comfortably follow. Unfortunately, his formal skill went with, and honed, an acuteness of observation, an objectivity that he applied to his inner and outer self as well as satirically to the world around him. In the 1940s, he tried to resolve this conflict by consulting psychologists. The experience with these less than successful consultations lies behind 'The psychiatrist's song' and several other poems where he seems to have hoisted the shrinks with their own petard. See 'The Psycho-analyst', 'The Psychiatrist speaks', and the compendious 'The neurotics'. (It is considered a possibility that consultation and treatment may have contributed to his relatively early death from a haemorrhage which might have been a result of electric shock therapy.)

The satirical strand in his work is rather dominant, excellent and also good teaching material. In my teaching days, his 'Man in the bowler hat', and 'Money' were in dozens of school anthologies along with that cat of his, and not only because anthologists cannibalize each other or have hidden agendas, no allusion intended. Anthologists were also fond of 'The British', and not merely on grounds of length, compared with 'England (Autumn 1938)', where the method of proceeding through binary ambivalences and oxymoron, with chorus-type, interjected verses, is perceptive and sharp but, in the end, it leaves the British and, of course, behind them Tessimond, in their tangles of compromise and disequilibrium between inner and outer forces.

For, in many ways, despite all the surface scintillation of his verse, a deep darkness lies under it and in its author: 'The solving emptiness that lies/ Just under all we do…' was never far from Tessimond's reach. Among many examples, see 'Cocoon for a skeleton', or 'Betrayal' which concludes: 'What panes of glass conceal our beating hearts.'

Tessimond, as a good formalist, is one of the highly memorable and quotable poets, a quality the reports that he was a good conversationalist would perhaps tend to support. He indulged in haunting night-life spots. This way of life was his whistling in the dark, as the pre-Mr-Bleaney aspects of 'Song in a saloon bar' suggest:

> Here we turn from shadows' questions –
>   Who we have been, will be, are –
> To the comfortable voices
>   Telling stories in the bar …

Yet he was avid for the life of the senses fully lived, even though mostly it was a city existence, and in his own unstructured way. See the posthumously collected 'Apologia' for some possible background on this.

His eye is not only objectively applied to inner and outer shades of camouflage, shiftiness and hypocrisy but also to the sensuous world:

> Grape-bloom of distant woods at dusk;
>   Storm-crown on Glaramara's head;
> The fire-rose over London night;
>   An old plough rusting autumn-red.

The third line of this extract from 'England (Autumn 1938)' is, weirdly, almost prophetic of the Blitz. His method here of using a wide focus to close in on a nub was a favourite device. The imagist clarity never entirely left him:

> The Round Pond is dimpled
>   only as much as
>   a girl's knee.

The poem 'Where', which one inevitably contrasts with Larkin's so different 'Here', is filled with exotic colour: 'While the sea spreads peacock feathers on cinnamon sands ...'

In a dramatic monologue with a long title, starting 'X while talking to a Professor ...' collected posthumously, X is discussing whether he should encourage his daughter to attend university and ends:

>   Shall she with this learned one
> Seek the dead? – or seek the living?
>   Light of lamp or light of sun?

Tessimond himself loved both lights but he was not enamoured of the student's light, the lamp that Yeats suggested came from the tomb. His satire 'A Man of culture', on the people who live books more than life, is a virtuoso set of variations on Pope's attack on Addison.

> Spying the coming man before he's come,
> He beats the first premonitory drum;
> Aware which reputation's almost dead,
> He plans the funeral speech a year ahead.

The next unexpected crossing of paths was in the early 1990s when friend and contemporary, Ian Hamilton, was preparing *The Oxford Companion to Twentieth-Century Poetry*. He showed me an impressive list of poets who, he thought, should be included and he wondered if I could think of any deserving names that had been overlooked. That list took some reading but I noticed Tessimond was missing. Almost inevitably, it seemed, I was offered the job of writing an entry on him. After Tessimond and I had criss-crossed each other for years, at last, we were figuratively to meet head on, though after those early encounters our routes had hardly run parallel like railway lines.

And here we are again. Is all good structure in a winding stair? The point has been reached where what was said in that entry should be expanded in retrospection.

Praised, or damned with the faintest praise, for being a 'formal' poet, clearly the concern for shaping is something I shared with Tessimond as well as the idea of dialogue mentioned above. Two minds is the least possible number for an intelligent person to be in, C. H. Sisson remarked somewhere. Duologue is the most succinct way to convey such things in verse. Tessimond was a dab hand at this and, fond of doing it economically, he was keen on the lyric of two quatrains. (Much of the Movement preferred three: thesis; antithesis; synthesis. Or the repetitious villanelle.) Tessimond leaves a poignant lack of synthesis to strike the reader for example, take 'Skaters' Waltz':

> '… So tempting to let freeze
>   One's deepest darkest pools
> And learn to skim with ease
>   Thin ice; for who but fools
>
> Dive into who knows what?'
>   'But if the ice by chance
> Breaks?' 'But if not, if not?
>   And how it glitters. Dance!'

– And that's how to maximise effects of enjambment. – See also 'Lovers' Conversation', a poignant twin quatrain, that must represent the thread of troubled relationships that run through his work, like a laddered stocking – in an image he would know. Most of his twin-quatrain poems are very effective.

His love poems are nearly all wishful or troubled. Two of the best and quietest are 'Not love perhaps' and 'Acknowledgement'.

Tessimond never reached resolution; he could never formalize the variousness of self and of the external world. And dissolution was always the old mole working away in his thought and work. A great deal of his unhappiness stemmed from his inability to form stable relationships with women, a problem that created the many shades of love poem in his work.

The last and probably least important thing you need to learn about an artist of any sort is a bit of biography. Arthur Seymour John Tessimond was born in 1902 and brought up in Birkenhead. His mother was probably of Welsh ancestry; his father was a bank inspector. An only child, he felt a sense of unloved loneliness. Sent to Charterhouse at fourteen, he ran away to London at sixteen, hoping to be a journalist – for which occupation he was temperamentally unsuited, let alone without any life experience. After a few weeks he ended up back in Birkenhead and from there went on to four years at Liverpool University.

There was an engagement to marry which eventually came to nothing and, in another love pursuit, he followed a woman friend to London, where, after various jobs, he ended up in advertising as a copy-writer, a job in which he stayed. His views of that activity are acutely and satirically recorded in several poems. He never managed satisfactory relationships with women and spent much of an inheritance from his father in 1945 on psychologists as mentioned above. After lying dead for two days, he was found in his flat on 15th May 1962 – dead of causes mentioned above. But he never doubted his poetry and his self-knowledge deserves the last word from the close of 'Soliloquy of the artists':

> We admire the cat not only
> For its independence but for its privacy:
> Contrive to be
> World-intimate and sedulously lonely: ...
>
> Call nothing sacrosanct:
> Spare none, not even ourselves: dissect
> All, ourselves most of all: nor expect,
> Save after our death, to be thanked.

And, at the back of that, in the wings, are Laforgue's Pierrots/Clowns of 'dandysme' – and perhaps not just formally.

Note:
This article is indebted to Hubert Nicholson for his edition *The Collected Poems of A. S. J. Tessimond*, Autolycus, 1985. The volume has been re-issued by Bloodaxe jointly with The Whiteknights Press, 2010.

Biographies

Timothy Adès is a translator-poet tending to use rhyme and metre. His books to date are: Victor Hugo *How to be a Grandfather* (Hearing Eye: a Complete Edition will follow) and two by Jean Cassou: *33 Sonnets* (Arc) and *The Madness of Amadis* (*Agenda* Editions). He translates Brecht and Sikelianós among others, and has awards for Cassou, Desnos, Hugo, and Alfonso Reyes. Much of his work is in periodicals or on the Brindin website.

Josephine Balmer's latest collection, *The Word for Sorrow*, was published by Salt in 2009. Previous collections and translations include *Chasing Catullus: Poems, Translations and Transgressions*, *Catullus: Poems of Love and Hate*, *Classical Women Poets* and *Sappho: Poems & Fragments*, all Bloodaxe. She has just completed a study of classical translation and poetry for Oxford University Press's 'Classical Presences' series.

Matthew Barton lives in Bristol and works as a writer, translator, editor and teacher of poetry and creative writing. His poems have appeared in a wide range of magazines, newspapers and anthologies, and he has also been featured twice on BBC Radio 4's 'Poetry Please'. Awards include BBC Wildlife Poet of the Year, a Hawthornden Fellowship, an Arts Council Writer's Award and second prize in the National Poetry Competition. Matthew Barton's two full-length collections are: *Learning to Row* (Peterloo 1999) and *Vessel* (Brodie Press 2009) which was reviewed in the previous 'Keenings' issue of *Agenda*.

Clare Best's poems are widely published in magazines including *The London Magazine*, *Resurgence*, *Magma*, T*he Rialto* and *The Warwick Review*. A chapbook, *Treasure Ground* (Happen*Stance* 2009), resulted from her residency at Woodlands Organic Farm on the Lincolnshire fens. Clare's first full collection, *Excisions*, came out from Waterloo Press in 2011. She teaches Creative Writing at Brighton University and is an Associate Lecturer for the Open University. She lives in Lewes

Alison Brackenbury's latest collection is *Singing in the Dark*, Carcanet, 2008. New poems can be read at her website: www.alisonbrackenbury.co.uk

Zoe Brigley's first collection *The Secret* (Bloodaxe, 2007) was very well received and was reviewed by Patricia McCarthy in the 'Notes for Broadsheet Poets' series. She is an Eric Gregory Award winner and her new collection, *Conquest*, will be reviewed in the next issue of *Agenda*. There was an in-depth interview with her by Peter Carpenter (also in this issue) in the Welsh issue of *Agenda*, 'Carpenters of Song' Vol 44, Nos 2-3., as well as some of her Bronte poems – inspired by a residency at the Bronte Parsonage – that are included in her new collection. Zoe comes from Wales, was a chosen young *Agenda* Broadsheet poet, and now lives in Pennsylvania with her husband and new baby.

Peter Carpenter has a 'New and Selected Poems', *Just Like That*, forthcoming from Smith/Doorstop in 2012, following five previous collections. He is a regular essayist and reviewer for *London Magazine* and *The North*. He co-directs Worple Press and has worked for many organisations including the Arvon Foundation, the Aldeburgh Poetry Festival and Survivors' Poetry. He was Creative Writing Fellow at the University of Reading during 2007-08, was made a Visiting Fellow at the University of Warwick in 2000, and has taught at Tonbridge School since 1992. He is the literary editor to William Curtis Hayward.

Phil Cohen is Emeritus Professor of Cultural Studies at the University of East London. *From the other side of the tracks: studies in narrative landscape* is due out from Palgrave Macmillan early next year. He had had poems published in *Critical Quarterly*, *Soundings*, and *Kites*.

D. V. Cooke (David Vincent Cooke) was born in Cheshire and graduated in English from London University. He worked for a number of years for The Poetry Library in London and has published in numerous poetry magazines including: *Acumen, Babel, Envoi, Frogmore Papers, Orbis, Outposts, Poetry Wales, Stand, Swansea Review, Tandem* and *Agenda*.

Peter Dale's most recent publications are *Peter Dale in Conversation with Cynthia Haven*, published by Between the Lines Press, *Under the Breath*, poems, and *Wry-Blue Loves,* a verse translation of Tristan Corbière, which received a Poetry Book Society Recommendation for Translation – both published by Anvil Press Poetry, as is his terza rima translation of *The Divine Comedy*, now going into its seventh edition. His translation of Paul Valéry, *Charms and Other Pieces*, Anvil, appeared in 2007 and is now in its second edition. His current book of verse is the sequence *Local Habitation,* 2009, also from Anvil who will publish his new book, *Diffractions: New and Collected Poems* in 2012. He now lives in Cardiff.

Robert Desnos (1900-45) was hailed by André Breton as 'the prophet of Surrealism'. Half his poems are in rhyme and metre, his touch often cavalier: translators tend to avoid these. He wrote love-poetry, children's poetry and songs and some magnificent long poems. During the Occupation he wrote great sequences: *Contrée, Andromède, Calixto*. Arrested as a Resistant, he was in Auschwitz and Buchenwald, became a slave labourer, and died at Terezin.

Roger Elkin's poetry has won over 150 Prizes and Awards internationally, including the Sylvia Plath Award for Poems about Women. His published collections include *Blood Brothers, New & Selected Poems* (2006), *No Laughing Matter* (2007), *Dog's Eye View* (2009), and *Fixing Things* (2011). Editor of *Envoi* magazine, (1991-2006), he received the *Howard Sergeant Memorial Award for Services to Poetry*. A published critic on Ted Hughes, Roger tutors Poetry at Wedgwood College, Barlaston, and was shortlisted for the Keele University Poetry Prize (2007).

June English has published three collections of poetry. *Counting the Spots* (Acumen, 2000) was shortlisted for the BBC 'New Voices' programme. *The Sorcerer's Arc* came out from Hearing Eye in 2004. Her latest collection is *Sunflower Equations* (Hearing Eye, 2008). She lives in Deal, Kent.

John Gladwell works part-time in Adult Education and has been published in a wide variety of magazines, including *PN Review, Stand, Staple, The Rialto, Ambit, London Magazine* and a previous edition of *Agenda*.

John A. Griffin was born in Tipperary, Ireland and lived for many years in St. Louis, MO, USA. He holds a BA from St. Louis University and read for his MA and PhD at Washington University, St Louis, where he specialized in German Idealist Philosophy and the work of Samuel Taylor Coleridge. He has had poems published in journals in the US and the UK. John currently lives and works in Riyadh, Saudi Arabia, where he teaches Literature and directs the English Language Academy for teachers.

Robert Hamberger has been awarded a Hawthornden Fellowship and shortlisted for a Forward prize. His poetry has been featured on the *Guardian* Poem of the Week website. His collections are *Warpaint Angel* (1997), *The Smug Bridegroom* (2002) and *Torso* (Redbeck, 2007.) He lives in Brighton.

Simon Jenner was born in Cuckfield, Sussex in 1959. He is Director of Survivors Poetry, and Waterloo Press. His books include two bi-lingual poetic debuts, *From Head to Foot* (K-Tek), *Player-Time* (Zeitriss), and *About Bloody Time, Wrong Evenings*, and *Pessoa* (Perdika). Another volume is forthcoming.

Jane Lovell lives in Rugby, Warwickshire and teaches at a nearby independent school. Her poems have been published in a range of journals including *Poetry Wales*, the *New Welsh Review*, *Envoi* and *Myslexia*. Threads of folklore and science run through her work.

Andrew McCulloch taught A Level English at a Sixth Form College in Cheshire for 27 years and is now a Lecturer in Education for the University of Huddersfield. His critical essays, reviews and poetry have appeared in *The English Review*, *PN Review* and the *TLS*.

Mc. Donald Ernest Dixon was born on the Caribbean Island of Saint Lucia has been actively involved with the arts, particularly the theatre from the early sixties. His first collection of poems, *Pebbles*, was published in 1973 and his work has appeared in several anthologies since, including *Agenda*. He has also published two novels, *Season of Mist and Misbegotten*, and a collection of short Stories – *Careme*. He is currently working on another novel, *Saints of Little Paradise*, which he hopes to complete by the end of the year.

Christine McNeill has published three poetry collections: *Kissing the Night* (Bloodaxe), *The Outsider* (Shoestring Press), and the latest *The Scent Gallery* (Shoestring Press, 2011). She has translated Rilke's poem-cycle *The Life of the Virgin Mary* (Dedalus Press), and with Patricia McCarthy co-translated Rilke's *The Book of Hours* (*Agenda* Editions). She is a tutor of German and creative writing, and lives in North Norfolk.

Inge Müller's maiden name was Meyer. Bombs falling on Berlin killed her parents and immured her in a cellar for three days. It is said that she never recovered. She had various jobs in East Germany, became a journalist, writer and poet, and worked with her third husband, playwright Heiner Müller.

William Oxley, born in Manchester, has worked as an accountant, gardener and actor. His poems have been widely published throughout the world in magazines and journals, and he has read his work on the UK and European radio. He has had many books of poetry published, including *Reclaiming the Lyre: New & Selected Poems* (Rockingham Press, 2001). He is consultant editor of *Acumen* magazine and co-founder of the Torbay Poetry Festival. His latest collection is *Sunlight in a Champagne Glass* (Rockingham Press, 2009). His work is featured on various websites including Anne Stewart's prestigious www.poetrypf.co.uk and www.creativetorbay.com.

Mandy Pannett works as a free-lance creative writing tutor. She has won prizes and been placed in competitions and her poetry has been published in international journals and anthologies. Recent work has been translated into German and Romanian. She has also acted as selecting editor for 'South' and been a judge of national poetry competitions. She has had three poetry collections published: *Bee Purple, Frost Hollow* (Oversteps Books) and *Allotments in the Orbital* (Searle Publishing) Her novella, *The Onion Stone*, was published in November 2011 by Pewter Rose Press.

Robin Renwick was born on a farm in Sussex and studied Design at the Royal College of Art. He has spent most of his working life as a designer/printer and lecturing in Art and Design. He retired from full time lecturing in 2001 and now works as a rock climbing instructor. He is previously unpublished.

Sue Roe is a poet, novelist and biographer who lives in Brighton. Her most recent books are *Gwen John: A Life* (Vintage) and *The Private Lives of the Impressionists* (Vintage), which has been translated into seven languages. Her book of poems, *The Spitfire Factory*, appeared in 1998 from Dale House Press. Her poetry is widely published in journals and anthologies including *New Poetries III* (Carcanet). She works with contemporary artists and has written exhibition catalogues for artists including Ellen Bell, Corinna Button, Marco Crivello and Anne Penman Sweet. She is a Senior Lecturer in Creative Studies at the University of Sussex.

Judith Shalan was born in Cambridge. After working for the BBC in London, for the Arabic Service and Radio Drama, she moved with her family to Kent and now lives in Sussex. She worked as press officer at Trinity Arts Centre in Tunbridge Wells, writing also for local papers, before joining Benn Publications as a journalist and later deputy editor, travelling widely in Britain and abroad. She has worked freelance as a sub editor for the last decade. This is the first time her poetry has been published.

Penelope Shuttle has lived in Cornwall since 1970 and is the widow of the poet, Peter Redgrove. She is the author of many collections of poems, and other books. Her latest collection, *Sandgrain and Hourglass* (Bloodaxe, 2010), was reviewed by Patricia McCarthy in the last 'Keenings' issue of *Agenda*. Her work can be heard on the Poetry Archive Website.

Robert Smith was born in London but now lives and works in Cambridge. He favours short forms, seeking for concentrated intensity of expression and sharp imagery. His work has previously been published in *Agenda*.

Will Stone, born 1966, is a poet, and literary translator who divides his time between England and Belgium. His first poetry collection *Glaciation* (Salt, 2007), won the international Glen Dimplex Award for poetry in 2008. A second collection *Drawing in Ash*, was published by Salt in May 2011 and won the 3am Magazine poetry book of the year award (2011). His published translations include *To The Silenced* – selected poems of Georg Trakl (Arc Publications, 2005) and *Journeys*, a collection of Stefan Zweig's European travel essays (Hesperus Press, 2010). His translations of long neglected Franco-Belgian poets Emile Verhaeren and Georges Rodenbach will be published by Arc in April 2012 and a first English translation of *Rilke in Paris* by Maurice Betz will appear from Hesperus Press in June 2012.

Leslie Tate is the author of two novels which portray modern love in different eras: *Frontliners* and *Aphrodite's Children*. He has a collection of love poems *Head and Heart*, published as an ebook/audiobook on Kindle and Itunes. He has also made a music/poetry recording *When Sparks Fly* which mixes his poems with music by award-winning composer Andrew McCrorie-Shand. See www.leslietate.com for details.

George Watson, who was born in 1927, is a Fellow of St John's College, Cambridge and author of *The Literary Critics, The Lost Literature of Socialism* and *Take Back the Past*. He edited the *New Cambridge Bibliography of English Literature*.

Robert Wells was born in Oxford in 1947. He has worked as a woodman, a teacher and in publishing. His verse translations of Virgil's *Georgics* and the *Idylls of Theocritus* were broadcast on Radio 3 and are included in his *Collected Poems and Translations*, published by Carcanet in 2009. He lives in France.

Bernard Robinson

1916-1944

Bernard was my mother's younger brother born in Sept 1916 in Widnes, Cheshire (formerly Lancashire) and he was studying Law when the War broke out. He joined the Lancashire Fusiliers and was on active service in Italy when he was killed early on in the Battle of Montecassino in May 1944. I'm not sure exactly when and where the poems were written but I have had them in my possession for several years now, along with other memorabilia (his last letter home, letter of condolence from the King, newspaper cutting telling of his death, photo of the cross marking his original grave) which my Aunt had carefully kept. Last month I went down to Montecassino to visit his grave; this I did partly for my mother who will be 100 in February and never managed to get there. It was, I think, the very moving experience of seeing his grave and so many other graves of young men that made me want to do something with his poems so that in some way his memory would live on. It would be particularly lovely if I was able to show my mother her brother's poems in print.

Charlotte Hosking

I come from ageless mystery

I come from ageless mystery
And I shall never die
From dawn to everlasting eve
I range the eternal sky.

Ask not why I am with you
Held in by mould of clay;
When death cuts clean these fetters
I'll take my ageless way.

Far beyond star and knowledge
Where time wields not his rod
I go my timeless journey
To the deathless halls of God.

Now for one timeless moment
My journey runs with time
Give me quick I beg of you
Some death-enduring sign.